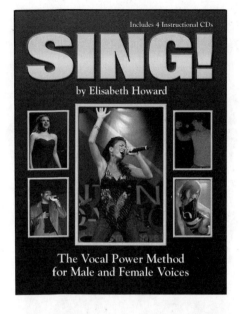

Includes 4 Instructional CDs

SING!

by Elisabeth Howard

The Vocal Power Method
for Male and Female Voices

The Elisabeth Howard Vocal Power Method of Singing has received praises from all over the world...

Exceptional presentation on commercial singing styles, movement for singers, small group master class and your insightful contributions to our various panel discussions. Your professionalism, depth of knowledge and commitment to NATS are truly exemplary."

Scott McCoy, NATS VP for Workshops
NATS/MTNA National Workshop Music Theater III April, 2005

"What I like about these CDs is their high-energy, business–like presentation; and the fact that both a treble and a male voice... are present in all the sung examples. What I really like is how well founded in reality the information is... none of the techniques advocated in the course are unhealthy, or unsupported;"

Journal of Singing, November/December 2000 National Association of Teachers of Singing

"Vocal Power is the consummate vocal method, giving the singer control of the instrument and versatility of style... the singer under-stands the whole spectrum of tools available in the singing voice."

Donna Hinds Sawyers
NATS/MTNA National Workshop Music Theater III April, 2005

"I never met somebody who not only knew but could analyze and explain and do singing like you did! I was absolutely fascinated! And you were so true when you showed what you meant!... This workshop was the greatest because with this knowledge you need not imitate a teacher but can find your own voice and way. And I hope very much to see you again as soon as possible."

Dr. Ursula Widmer, Mozarteum Innsbruck, Austria, June 2001

"Elisabeth Howard's Vocal Power Method is so comprehensive that you will receive more in one sitting than you will with most teachers in a year's worth of instruction."

Laurie Lee Cosby
NATS/MTNA National Workshop Music Theater III April, 2005

"I want to really thank you for the wonderful workshop you did here in Brescia. Everyone I spoke to was so enthusiastic about your work and the "power" you bring it out with... I had to get you here in Italy in one way or another and I did. All the struggle I went through God only knows but the effort was worth it."

Anna Gotti, promoter, singer, voice teacher,
Vice President of AICI, workshop, Brescia Jazz Festival, Italy and Associazione Insegnanti di Canto Italiana - A.I.C.I. June 2001

"...The workshop was very successful... The Seminar was also attended by several pop and jazz teachers. ... The students were enthusiastic and are awaiting her to come back for the next Seminar."

Donatella Luttazzi, translator, singer, Rome, Italy workshop - Scuola Popolare di Musica del Testaccio in collaboration with Associazione Insegnanti di Canto Italiana, (AICI), May 2002

"A great teacher and a professional singer who loves to sing and has the great power to make people fall in love with singing. A charismatic lady who can transfer all the energy and the enthusiasm and the know-how from her to each student, making it easy to understand even the most difficult technique, following you step by step until it becomes part of you.... The workshop she presented in Rome taught me a lot about music, vocal techniques, exercises to improve my singing. Even in such a short time through her original and effective teaching methods I received so many hints and help me clear up my path leading to the healthy use of my voice and make me want to go on singing. Thanks, Elisabeth!"

Laura Albanese, student, Rome, Italy
Scuola Popolare di Musica del Testaccio in collaboration with Associazione Insegnanti di Canto Italiana, (AICI), May 2002

"...you fascinated us all. So let me say that I am proud that your workshop succeeded very well. The students were all very happy and so were the teachers who were there."

Giuppi Paone, professional singer,
Vice President of Il Testaccio, Rome, Italy Scuola Popolare di Musica del Testaccio in collaboration with Associazione Insegnanti di Canto Italiana, (AICI), May 2002

"Recently, I taught a choir to produce the four resonances you describe in Born To Sing. In fifteen minutes they were producing a fuller, richer sound than their choir director had ever heard before. Your teaching methods are highly original and effective."

John Glenn Paton, editor 26 Italian Art Songs and Arias-Alfred Publishing; Emeritus Professor of Music, University of Colorado, Lecturer, USC

"You illustrated the popular styles with clarity and authority. I thought it was one of the best sessions".

Oren Brown, Voice Faculty Emeritus, The Juilliard School, former Lecturer in Voice Therapy, Washington University School of Medicine, NATS National Convention, Philadelphia, July 2000

"We were most fortunate to have this dynamic, talented lady share with us her many years of experience in bringing out the hidden and not-so-hidden singer within. In a most amazing manner, Ms. Howard brings people up on stage and makes the most profound changes in their styles, abilities and total presentation.... This brilliant woman's well-developed methods produce unbelievable results. The fact that she knows how to break down every singing style into bits and pieces that anyone can understand and put into practical use seems unprecedented in my experience. Many of our members have said they would love to repeat the experience.

Judy Lamppu, singer, song writer, Board of Directors, LA Women in Music, August, 2002

SING!

Elisabeth Howards' Vocal Power Method of Singing has received
praises from all over the world...

*"To my friend Elisabeth,
Thank you for your invaluable help."
Love,
Sting*

"Exceptional presentation on commercial singing styles, movement for singers, small group master class and your insightful contributions to our various panel discussions. Your professionalism, depth of knowledge and commitment to NATS are truly exemplary."

*Scott McCoy, NATS VP for Workshops
NATS/MTNA National Workshop Music Theater III
April, 2005*

"What I like about these CDs is their high-energy, business-like presentation; and the fact that both a treble and a male voice...are present in all the sung examples. What I really like is how well founded in reality the information is... none of the techniques advocated in the course are unhealthy, or unsupported;"

*Journal of Singing, November/December 2000
National Association of Teachers of Singing*

"I never met somebody who not only knew but could analyze and explain and do singing like you did! I was absolutely fascinated! And you were so true when you showed what you meant!...This workshop was the greatest because with this knowledge you need not imitate a teacher but can find your own voice and way. And I hope very much to see you again as soon as possible."

*Dr. Ursula Widmer, Mozarteum Innsbruck,
Austria, June 2001*

"Elisabeth Howard's Vocal Power Method is so comprehensive that you will receive more in one sitting than you will with most teachers in a year's worth of instruction."

*Laurie Lee Cosby NATS/MTNA National
Workshop Music Theater III April, 2005*

"I want to really thank you for the wonderful workshop you did here in Brescia. Everyone I spoke to was so enthusiastic about your work and the "power" you bring it out with...I had to get you here in Italy in one way or another and I did. All the struggle I went through God only knows but the effort was worth it."

*Anna Gotti, promoter, singer, voice teacher,
Vice President of AICI, workshop,
Brescia Jazz Festival, Italy and Associazione
Insegnanti di Canto Italiana—A.I.C.I. June 2001*

"...The workshop was very successful... The Seminar was also attended by several pop and jazz teachers...The students were enthusiastic and are awaiting her to come back for the next Seminar."

*Donatella Luttazzi, translator, singer,
Rome, Italy workshop—Scuola Popolare di
Musica del Testaccio in collaboration with
Associazione Insegnanti di Canto Italiana,
(AICI), May 2002*

"...you fascinated us all. So let me say that I am proud that your workshop succeeded very well. The students were all very happy and so were the teachers who were there."

*Giuppi Paone, professional singer, Vice President of
Il Testaccio, Rome, Italy Scuola Popolare di Musica
del Testaccio in collaboration with Associazione
Insegnanti di Canto Italiana, (AICI), May 2002*

"Recently, I taught a choir to produce the four resonances you describe in Born To Sing. In fifteen minutes they were producing a fuller, richer sound than their choir director had ever heard before. Your teaching methods are highly original and effective."

*John Glenn Paton, editor 26 Italian Art Songs and
Arias-Alfred Publishing; Emeritus Professor of Music,
University of Colorado, Lecturer, USC*

"You illustrated the popular styles with clarity and authority. I thought it was one of the best sessions."

*Oren Brown, Voice Faculty Emeritus,
The Juilliard School, former Lecturer in Voice Therapy,
Washington University School of Medicine,
NATS National Convention, Philadelphia, July 2000*

"The use of the "Mix" has been rewarding for my students and "smoothed out" the "bumps and glitches" that a singer of pop music can often experience. Your demonstration and application of putting the soul/feel back into music left us all breathless and very motivated."

*Tracy Canini, ANATS member,
Australia National Association of Teachers
of Singing National Conference 1997*

"Vocal Power is the consummate vocal method, giving the singer control of the instrument and versatility of style...the singer understands the whole spectrum of tools available in the singing voice."

*Donna Hinds Sawyers NATS/MTNA National
Workshop Music Theater III April, 2005*

"A resounding 'thank you' from your friends at NATS Victoria and Vancouver, B. C. Canada for an energetic and exciting workshop. Liz, you lovingly gave each singer such quality attention and they in turn responded well to your techniques... Witnessing your open approach, we better understand the stylistic differences that the repertoire of music theatre, pop, blues, jazz and country demands. With these tools, I know many of us now feel ready to take more artistic risks that will allow each singer to make each song their own. Please come again!"

Signi Murgatroy, President, NATS Victoria Chapter, November 2002

"Elisabeth Howard demonstrates fantastically, really goes deep into technique, analyzes it like I have never ever heard anybody do it and is so clear about technical concepts, that you really have a tool in your hands when you leave this workshop...Actually I find her also good for teaching teachers, (the way she can analyze and come to the point in a very short time, how she finds solutions being critical and supportive at the same time is a lesson in itself for every teacher, not only singers)...I am definitely planning to invite her again...The pianist who accompanied the course said to me: 'You know, she is a pedagogical genius, and even if you don't want to learn about singing, you can learn so much about teaching'...!"

Magdalena Pattis, Voice Faculty, Program Coordinator, Mozarteum Innsbruck, Austria, June 2001

"Elisabeth Howard and Vocal Power presented a wonderful master class for California State University, Fullerton. With her comprehensive understanding of vocal pedagogy and technique, she achieved instantaneous results with the students. Her approach to the "mysteries" of vibrato was very enlightening and, nearly nine years later, I am still using several of the vocalizes she introduced in this session."

Dr. Mark Goodrich, Voice Faculty, California State University, Fullerton

"There are major differences between classical and non-classical vocal technique and style. Liz Howard knows those differences and knows how to teach both very effectively."

Robert Edwin, NATS member, "The Bach to Rock Connection" column for NATS Journal, NATS National Treasurer; NATS National Convention, Philadelphia, July 2000

"She manages every subject with skill and knowledge and is very prepared from the musical and scientific point of view, in each and every style. With generosity, she gave examples with her own voice, and did not save her fatigue. I am a singing teacher in classical and opera music and member of AICI. It was a very nice experience, that opened up my horizons and enriched my knowledge."

"Meeting Elisabeth Howard" by Ersilia Colonna, excerpt from review of workshop, Brescia Jazz Festival, co-sponsored with Associazione Insegnanti di Canto Italiana (AICI) June 2001

"Yet again, another outstanding job! We are so fortunate to have had you give us this generous, loving and incredibly helpful experience today. I've been using your resonance terminology and techniques with wonderful success...You are just delightful, and of great benefit to all 14 of my students of my studio that attended—including ME!!"

Diann Alexander, Voice Faculty Pepperdine University and California State Lutheran University, Board of Directors, NATS/LA Chapter, Los Angeles workshop for NATS/LA chapter, January 2001

"Your presentation in San Francisco was great, but not long enough! 1 was amazed by your own ability to sing in so many different styles, as well as impressed by the sounds of some of your students who sang on tape. I hope we can have you back again to do a master class with students singing various styles...or a longer, more indepth presentation for teachers."

Connie Venti, MTAC Voice Chair South Music Teachers Association of California, State Convention, San Francisco, California, July 2001

"Thank you so much for your wonderful and exciting presentation on Popular Singing at our convention. The audience was delighted and thrilled to hear someone who could sing as well as teach all of the various styles you were presenting. People were also very impressed with the results you were able to achieve with our singers that day. I'm very happy that we were able to expose our attendees to the many talented and gifted teachers like you in our organization".

Thomas Faracco, Program Chair, 46th NATS National Convention Philadelphia, July 2000

"Elisabeth Howard presented a master class last July at the NATS National Convention in Philadelphia, and everyone was impressed by her radiant positive energy, her quick zeroing-in on the technical needs of the students, and her chameleon-like, from classical to pop, blues and country styles."

NATS Journal of Singing—review by Susan Larson, NATS National Convention, Philadelphia, July 2000

"Thank you so much for your wonderful session at the ANATS Conference. I found the whole afternoon very stimulating. Of particular interest was your work on vibrato—that was fantastic! Also the fact that you have had such success with very young singers is making me re-think my whole approach to "starting" ages. One afternoon just wasn't enough. I sincerely hope I have the chance of working with you again—please come back soon!"

Elizabeth Pascoe, ANATS member, Voice Faculty, WA Academy of Performing Arts, Edith Cowan University, Perth, Western Australia, Australia National Association of Teachers of Singing National Conference 1997

"Making a grand entrance in true diva style, to the tune of "It Don't' Mean A Thing If You Ain't Got That Swing", Elisabeth Howard took charge of the next section, displaying her credentials through the PA system in no uncertain terms. "Yeah, I wanna sing like that!" Demonstrating her Vocal Power technique, she touched on the roots of vocal style, explaining how blues and jazz scales were an essential part of improvisation, and provided insight to how songs in any genre can be approached for maximum impact. Following that, Elisabeth guided everyone there through a series of exercises. Even the bartenders and security guards got into it! The differences were immediately apparent as each exercise was done."

Review by Jim Yamagishi "Vocal Mecca" at the Knitting Factory—Hollywood, July 12, 2003

For my husband, Geoff... my reason, my life.

Note: All vocal exercises are designed for use with a healthy voice. They are intended to keep your voice healthy and to improve your level of singing. If you think you may have vocal problems, immediately consult a voice teacher or a laryngologist.

Cover Photos: (Clockwise from left) Devon Guthrie (Photo: Howard Passamanick Photography), Hadas, Tanner Redman, Sarah Hudson and Chauncey Isom

Published in the United States of America by Vocal Power, Inc.

Exclusively distributed by Alfred Publishing Co., Inc.

For more information contact:
Vocal Power Academy
2123 N. Topanga Canyon Blvd.
Topanga, CA 90290
800-829-SONG (7664)
e-mail: lizhoward@vocalpowerinc.com
Website: www.vocalpowerinc.com

Quote from *Great Singers on Great Singing* by Jerome Hines
by permission of Doubleday & Company, Inc.

Special thanks to John Glenn Paton and Joan Thompson for help with this book's editing.

Piano accompaniments by Elisabeth Howard

Additional material in chapters on Breathing and Support
by Geoffrey G. Forward

Musical Graphics by Skip Perkins Music Preparation

Cover and Book Design by Accolade Graphics

Also by Elisabeth Howard:

ABC's of Vocal Harmony (Book and 4 CDs)

Born to Sing DVD by Elisabeth Howard and Howard Austin

SING! with 4 CDs

ISBN 0-934419-18-3

SING! with 4 CDs and DVD
ISBN 0-934419-19-1

Table of Contents

Vocal Technique

SING!

*"This training has carried me through years of
healthy, professional singing."*

Paige O'Hara
Voice of "Belle" in the film "Beauty and the Beast"
Eponine in "Les Miserables" on Broadway

Vocal
Technique

CHAPTER ONE

Breathing

"I am impressed with Elisabeth Howard's wonderful approach of non-classic style of singing... She is the first pedagogue to give coherent explanations about the technique necessary to these kinds of singers..."

Paolo Zedda
Ph.D.: Sorbonne/Paris; Vocal instructor: Paris Conservatoire Supérieur

(Singing Techniques CD, Tracks 1-3)

If we approach the voice as if it were an instrument, we see that it has characteristics of both a wind instrument and a stringed instrument. The sound produced on a wind instrument, such as the flute or clarinet, is created by air (breath) flow and air (breath) pressure. This is also true of your voice, which uses your breath flow and breath pressure to make sound. The sound produced on a stringed instrument, such as the violin, is started by the vibration of the strings and enhanced or resonated in the body of the instrument. This is also true of your voice. Your vocal folds (vocal cords) vibrate, creating a sound which then resonates in the area from your vocal folds to your lips, called the vocal tract.

To play this instrument, your voice, you need breath control and breath support. As a singer, it is important that you learn how to take easy, full breaths. Refilling your lungs completely gives you a number of great advantages. You are able to sing longer phrases. You have increased control for singing high and low notes, for singing softly and loudly and for tone coloring and for flexibility. It helps you to control your vibrato, to speed it up or slow it down or to sing a straight tone (no vibrato). Proper breath management and support helps you to sing a clear tone and aids in singing smoothly through the registers.

How You Breathe

I want to assure you that breathing and support is not a complicated process. It happens naturally, it's easy to do, and it is simple to understand and so I am going to use very simple, basic terms and images.

There are three sets of muscles involved in breathing and support for voice:
1. The diaphragm,
2. The rib muscles, and
3. The abdominal muscles.

SING!

Rib Cage, Diaphragm and Abdomen

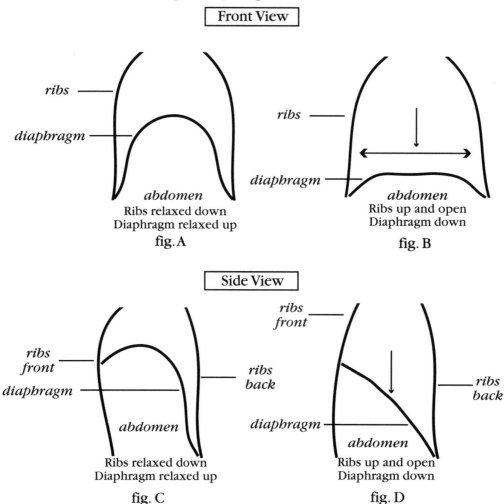

Front View

fig. A
Ribs relaxed down
Diaphragm relaxed up

fig. B
Ribs up and open
Diaphragm down

Side View

fig. C
Ribs relaxed down
Diaphragm relaxed up

fig. D
Ribs up and open
Diaphragm down

The above diagram is a good, simple representation of the breathing mechanism. If you would like to know more of the physiological terminology and exact photos and drawings, you can find it in the following books: *Singing, the Mechanism and the Technic,* by William Vennard; *The Science of Vocal Pedagogy,* by D. Ralph Appelman; *The Science of the Singing Voice,* by Johan Sundberg, *Your Voice: An Inside View,* by Scott McCoy, DM.

First, you need a clear understanding of what these muscles look like and what they feel like when you breathe. Simplify your study by looking at only one set of muscles at a time. Study the drawings above and follow the explanation in the next section until you have such a clear idea of how your breathing works that you can explain it to yourself without referring to the book. Start with the ribs. Then go on to the diaphragm and finally the abdominal muscles.

The body tries to do whatever the mind images. So you must have an accurate idea of what your rib muscles, diaphragm, and abdominal muscles are doing when you breathe. In the next section, we will take a detailed look at how these muscles work.

But first... people sometimes confuse the diaphragm and the abdominal muscles, so let's make the difference clear.

Let's look at the abdominal muscles first, because they are the easiest to identify. The abdominal muscles are the muscles around your waist, in the front, on the sides and around your back. You can feel them with your fingers.

Do this: Place your hands on your waist, with your thumbs toward the back, in the soft area between your ribs and your hips. Push in with your hands a little bit, so you know you are there. Now cough gently. What did you feel happening under your hands? Do it again. You feel the muscles under your hands getting firm and pushing slightly. Those are your abdominal muscles. They are on the outside of your body and you can feel them moving. When supporting for singing, these muscles must be kept flexible and never tense.

Now let's look at the diaphragmatic muscle. Let's look at its shape first, then where it is in your body. The diaphragm is composed of muscles and tendons. Think of it as being thin and round, like a pancake. Now think of placing a bowl upside down on the table and draping the pancake over the upside down bowl. Do you see that there is a dome shape to both the bowl and the pancake? Now imagine that the bowl is taken away, but the pancake (your diaphragm) remains in the dome shape. This is the shape of the diaphragm in figure A and C in the above drawing. This dome shape is the natural position of your diaphragm. It likes this shape. Whenever it is moved out of this shape, it goes back to the dome shape as soon as it can. Sort of like a rubber ball that you squeeze, but when you let it go, it goes back to its round shape.

Now let's look at where the diaphragm is in your body. You know that you have lungs in your chest area and that you have intestines down lower, in your stomach, or abdominal area. Think of this dome shaped diaphragm as separating your intestines from your lungs. Your diaphragm is inside your body, still in its dome shape, with the edges of the dome sealed to your ribs all the way around. The dome comes up slightly into your chest cavity. Sometimes the diaphragm is called the floor of your chest cavity and the ceiling of your intestinal cavity.

To get more specific with this imagery, the edges of your diaphragm are connected to the edges of your ribs all the way around. If you feel the edges of your ribs, starting in the front, you can feel that the edges of your ribs go lower as you move around the sides and to your back. In fact, in your back the ribs go way down to the small of your back. The diaphragmatic muscle is connected low in your back.

A quick side-bar: Your lungs go all the way down into the small of your back where you can feel the edges of your ribs.

Breathing

To make sound, we have to breathe in (inhale) first. So let's take a look at how we inhale.

There are two sets of muscles involved in inhalation, the rib muscles and the diaphragmatic muscle (see p. 12, figures A,B,C,D). The abdominal muscles are not muscles of inhalation. They should be relaxed as you breathe in.

In this discussion, I am going to substitute "ribs" for "rib muscles." The muscles between the ribs are called "intercostal muscles." We all know that the ribs don't move without the rib muscles, so it is easier to refer to just "ribs."

When you breathe naturally, your ribs and your diaphragm operate together. But for purposes of examination, it is simpler to separate them, look at each one, get control over each, and then put them back together.

Why does the air move into your lungs when you expand your ribs? It is simple. When you expand your ribs, you create a larger space inside your chest cavity. This creates a lower air pressure, or a partial vacuum, inside your chest cavity. The air outside, which is under higher pressure, rushes in to equalize the air pressure. You don't have to understand the physics of breathing to breathe. Just be aware that it happens in a natural way.

What you do need to understand, however, is that *the air coming in does not expand your ribs. It is your expansion of your ribs that causes the air to come in*. Get a clear picture

SING!

of that concept and you will never struggle for breath. All you have to do is open your ribs and the breath comes in. Easy!

1. Rib Breathing Exercise

Let's look at how you breathe with your ribs.

When you want to take a breath in (inhale), your lower ribs expand on the sides, in the front, and in the back. Actually, there is an upward and outward movement of your ribs (look at p. 12, figures B, D). When you want to let your breath out (exhale), your lower ribs lower back down and you can feel that they move slightly in (look at p. 12, figures A, C). This is their position of rest.

Try that. Open your ribs on the sides, back and front, and feel the air coming in. Hold your ribs open for a moment. Feel that the air does not go in or out. Now lower your ribs and feel the air go out.

Notice that when you lower your ribs, you don't have to pull them down. Gravity pulls your ribs down. All you have to do is stop holding them up and allow them to move down. Notice, also, that you can allow your ribs to lower as quickly or as slowly as you want.

2. Rib Breathing Exercise

Expand your ribs. Now let them go all at once. Expand your ribs again. Now lower them slowly. You have control over how quickly or slowly you lower your ribs.

Your upper chest, also ribs, should remain in repose, not lifting as you breathe. Or at least not lifting much.

3. Rib Breathing Exercise

Let's do an exercise that will help you keep your upper chest in a state of dynamic relaxation. Your upper chest must be up and open, not collapsed, for a powerful and expressive voice. This is necessary for healthy, natural breathing and rich, full resonance.

The position of your upper chest is actually controlled by your upper spine. Feel what happens to your upper chest when you let your upper spine slump over. Ready. Slump. Your upper ribs collapse down and in. Now straighten your upper back. Ready. Straighten. Your chest comes up and open. Let this position feel natural and comfortable, not stiff or forced.

Don't obstruct the breath passages by closing your mouth and lips or bunching up your tongue and pulling it back in your throat. When your breath passages are wide open, your breathing is practically silent. If you can hear yourself breathe, you're restricting the flow.

If You Get Dizzy

If you begin to get dizzy as you do the breathing exercises, stop and allow the dizziness to pass. It is just that you are getting more oxygen than you are used to. When your body gets used to more oxygen, you won't get dizzy. If your throat gets dry, swallow or drink some water.

4. Rib Breathing Exercise

Feel your chest up and open. Feel your breathing passages free. Think into the lower ribs at your sides and in your back and expand them wide. Feel the expansion drawing air into your lungs. Feel the air cooling your breath passages. Hold the expansion for a moment, without closing your throat. Keep your abdomen relaxed. And now lower your ribs, without collapsing your upper chest. And feel the air moving out and warming your breathing passages.

Again. Expand the lower ribs. Feel the movement start in your lower back, along your spine. Feel the air coming in. And lower your ribs. Don't collapse the upper chest. Feel the air going out. And relax.

Don't lift your shoulders or upper chest as your expand your ribs. Expand… Relax your shoulders down. And lower your ribs. Don't collapse your upper chest. Expand. And lower. Expand. Shoulders down. And lower your ribs. Don't collapse. Expand. And lower. Relax.

As you do this exercise, it's helpful to watch yourself in a mirror.

Again. This time stretch your ribs as wide as they can go. Ready. Expand. More. Shoulders down. And lower your ribs. Control the lowering. Expand. Shoulders down. Lower. Don't just drop the ribs. Expand. Shoulders down. Lower. Don't collapse. Expand. And lower. Relax.

If you feel any dizziness, stop doing the exercise and wait till it passes.

Once you are used to the movement, go for speed and ease, starting slowly at first and gradually getting faster. Ready. Expand. And lower. Expand. And lower… Shoulders down. Expand. Lower. Expand. Neck relaxed. Lower. Expand. Free and easy. Expand. Lower. Expand. Lower. Expand. Lower. Expand. Lower. Relax.

After only a few days of doing the rib breathing exercise, you'll find your ribs are flexible enough to expand easily to their limit.

5. Rib Breathing Exercise

Expand your ribs on one count. Then lower your ribs on four counts. You can use a "sssss" against your teeth to feel the resistance of the air pressure. Expand on one count, lower on six counts. Expand on one count, lower on eight counts. Expand on one count, lower on ten counts. And so on. Lengthen the number of counts on exhalation as far as you want to.

Lower Back Breathing

As the ribs expand, the lower back muscles just above the waist should also expand for maximum intake of air.

Lower Back and Rib Exercise

1. Clasp your hands above you and exhale as you slowly lean forward with your hands still clasped.
2. Come up slowly as you inhale, feeling the widening of the lower ribs and lower back.
3. Without stopping the air flow, hiss out your air slowly, feeling your ribs resisting, slowly returning to their original position.
4. You can practice this with singing phrases as well.

Diaphragmatic Breathing

Now let's take a look at how the diaphragm works. Remember that its normal position is a dome shape. Its edges are connected to your lower ribs all the way around. The diaphragm does not have any sensory nerve endings that allow you to feel the diaphragm or its movement. But you can feel what happens around the diaphragm when it moves, so you can tell it is moving.

When you want to breathe in, your diaphragm flattens its dome shape. So in effect, it moves down. (Look at figures B and D in the drawing on p. 12.) This creates more space in your chest cavity.

When you create this extra space in your chest cavity, you create a lower air pressure, or partial vacuum, in your chest cavity. The air outside is under higher pressure, so it rushes into your lungs to equalize the air pressure.

It is important to visualize the sequence correctly. **It is your diaphragm moving down**

that draws in the air, not the air that pushes your diaphragm down.

When your diaphragm moves down, it pushes against and compresses your intestines. The pressure on the intestines causes them to push out against your abdominal muscles (p. 12, fig. B and D). So even though you can't actually feel your diaphragm moving, you can feel pressures in your waist area and you can see your waist moving out as the air comes in.

To exhale, you just release your diaphragm. It will rise by itself to its normal dome shape. As it comes up, it puts the air in your chest (lungs) under higher pressure, so some of the air moves out of your lungs.

1. Diaphragm Breathing Exercise

Here is a good exercise to feel the sensations of diaphragmatic breathing.

Lie down on your back. Let yourself go completely relaxed. Imagine you are in a wonderful place where there are no worries, no troubles, no cares. In your imagination see what the place looks like, hear the sounds there, feel the temperature, smell the air. Spend 30 seconds, a minute, or longer, just experiencing the place in your mind.

As you breathe the air in, feel it cooling your mouth and throat. How far down the breathing passage can you feel it cooling? As the air comes out, feel it warming up those areas that it cooled.

Now, without changing anything, flop one hand on your stomach, over your belly button. As you breathe in, feel which direction your hand moves, up or down. As you breathe out, feel which direction your hand moves, up or down.

When you breathe diaphragmatically, as you breathe in, your abdomen expands, so your hand is moved up. As you breathe out, your abdomen drops back down, so your hand moves down.

You don't have to make your abdomen expand or move down, it happens naturally, as a result of the movement of your diaphragm. The muscles of your abdomen should stay completely relaxed.

Feel what it feels like in your waist area as you are doing this exercise. Remember that feeling.

Next, stand up and recreate the exercise in a standing position. Feel the same expansion around your waist as you breathe in, and your waist coming back in as the air goes out.

If you are not used to breathing with your diaphragm, it may take a few daily sessions, maybe a couple of weeks, to be able to breathe diaphragmatically in a standing position.

Exercise Note: When your abdominal muscles are tense, it's difficult to breathe. You can feel this. Tense your abdomen, as if you're going to be hit in the stomach. Ready. Tense. Hold it and try to take a deep breath. It's hard to do. Now relax your abdominals and take a deep breath. Much easier.

2. Diaphragm Breathing Exercise

First, put your hands on your waist in the soft area between your ribs and your hips. Now expand your ribs about half-way and hold them in that position. Breathe in without lifting the ribs any further. Feel the expansion all around your waist. This is the result of your diaphragm moving down. Now breathe out, without lowering your ribs. Feel your waist relax in, but don't intentionally pull in. Your waist comes back in because your diaphragm goes back up into its dome shape. Again, with the ribs half-way expanded, breathe in. Feel the expansion around your waist. Breathe out, without lowering your ribs. Feel your waist relax in. And relax.

Diaphragmatic breathing feels like it brings the air deep into the small of your back. Let's take a diaphragmatic breath and feel the expansion in the lower back. Ribs up half-way. Take a diaphragmatic breath in. Feel the expansion in your waist, under your thumbs. And breathe out, keeping your ribs up. In. Breathe into your lower back. And out. In… and out. In… and out. Relax.

3. Diaphragm Breathing Exercise

Now for a little more ease and freedom. Let's do a rapid breathing or panting exercise. This will strengthen your diaphragmatic muscle and make it more flexible. It's helpful to watch yourself in a mirror as you do it.

Ready. Keep your ribs expanded about half-way and your breathing passages open. Breathe in and out. In. Out. In. Out. Let your breathing be smooth and free. Relax.

If you feel any dizziness, stop doing the exercise until it passes. Swallow or drink some water if your throat gets dry.

Now we'll go even faster. Ready. Expand your ribs. In. Out. In. Out. (panting). Relax.

Now, as fast as you can.

As you practice the panting exercise, breathe in as far as you can each time and go only as fast as you can without losing control.

Intake of Air

The nose breath or the mouth breath? I recommend intake of air through your mouth only, or with some nose breath at the same time rather than only a nose breath with the lips closed, for the following reasons:

1. You can take a fuller and faster breath through your mouth than you can through your nose alone.

2. Taking a fast breath through your nose alone is noisy and distracting.

3. If you have a cold, it may be impossible to breathe through your nose.

4. Breathing through your mouth opens the vocal tract and prepares it for singing.

Of course, if you choose to, you may breathe through your nose when you have time, such as during the introduction of the song or during a musical interlude ("break").

Don't hold your breath before you sing. Holding your breath tends to tighten your throat muscles. Take a free, easy breath just before you sing. If you do get into the situation where you must hold the air for any reason, hold it with a relaxed throat. Just keep your ribs expanded and your diaphragm down.

Guidelines:

1. Your intake of air should be deep, natural, and effortless.

2. Your audience should not be distracted by your breathing.

3. Keep your upper chest up and open and your shoulders relaxed as you take a breath. Raising your shoulders looks awkward and causes tensions in your throat.

4. Never pull your stomach up and in as you breathe. Pulling up and in restricts the downward expansion of the lungs and inhibits natural support.

Exercises

1. Begin by taking a full breath (√). Using the teeth as resistance against the air pressure, hiss out for the duration of 1 count. Replenish the air in 1 count. Hiss out for 2 counts. Take back what you have used in 1 count. Hiss out for 3 counts. Replenish in 1 count and so on. Keep the air pressure steady. You should be able to reach the count of 10, always replenishing in 1 count and keeping a steady flow.

SING!

(Singing Techniques CD Tracks 2-3)

In, 2   out...... .2...... .3.........4........
(√........)   (s s s s s s s s s s s s s s s s s)

In, 2   out...... .2...... .3.........4........
(√........)   (s s s s s s s s s s s s s s s s s)

In, 2   out...... .2...... .3.........4........
(√........)   (s s s s s s s s s s s s s s s s s)

2. Try the same exercise with a soft hiss, keeping the air pressure steady. Keep a steady flow. In-out-in-out. Keep your shoulders relaxed and down. Do not raise them to help you breathe in. Feel your neck and jaw relaxed. Your tongue should be relaxed in your mouth, not pulled down. The tip of your tongue should rest against the back of your lower teeth. Feel a slight yawning sensation as you feel the air flowing in through both your mouth and nose to cool the back of your throat.

In, 2   out...... .2...... .3.........4........
(√........)   (s s s s s s s s s s s s s s s s s)

In, 2   out...... .2...... .3.........4........
(√........)   (s s s s s s s s s s s s s s s s s)

In, 2   out...... .2...... .3.........4........
(√........)   (s s s s s s s s s s s s s s s s s)

CHAPTER TWO

Support

"Working with Liz has provided a tremendous boost to my vocal range, technical proficiency and performance skills... I only wish I had started with her two years earlier. I'd have been so much further along."

Tanner Richie
Actor/Singer, "Les Miserables" National Tour; Nip/Tuck, Threshold

(Singing Techniques CD, Tracks 4-5)

Breath Support

In this discussion of breath support, let's first talk about the breath, without the complication of also creating sound. When you understand how to consciously control your breath support by itself, it will be much easier to control it when you make sound.

Breath support refers to the outflow (exhalation) of air from your lungs. We use breath support in normal breathing, in whistling, in blowing up a balloon, in lifting something heavy, in laughing, in coughing, and so on. Kids use breath support when they call to one another in the playground. Babies use it when they cry. Breath support is a natural activity for the body. But it is an unconscious activity. You probably are not aware of creating breath support or how your body is creating it.

Consciously controlling breath support becomes a lot easier once you realize that your body already knows how to do it. Breath support is a mystery or a problem only when you are not aware of how you do it. Once you understand how your body naturally creates breath support, you will be able to easily and consciously recreate what your body does unconsciously.

So let's take a look at how your body naturally creates breath support. We'll examine it from the standpoint of two extremes. At the one extreme, we use very little breath support, which feels like we are doing nothing at all. On the other end of the spectrum, we use very strong breath support, which takes an effort.

Controlled Breath Support

When you want to slowly let your breath out in a relaxed manner, it feels like you don't use any energy to release it. In reality, gravity is pulling down on your ribs and you are controlling the outflow by keeping your ribs expanded and slowly allowing them to lower. (Remember how we explained rib breathing in Chapter One.) At the same time, your diaphragm is trying to rise to its dome shape. You are keeping it down and slowly allowing it to rise. (See the explanation of diaphragmatic breathing in Chapter One.) So you are using a little energy. We need to identify this process, so let's call it "controlled breath support."

1. Controlled Breath Support Exercise

You can feel controlled breath support. Just for this exercise, it is easier to feel and control the outflow or air if you release the air on an "sssssssss." Take a breath, expanding the ribs, lower back and diaphragm, and slowly let your air out on ten counts. Feel how easy and relaxed that is?

As a contrast, take a big, power breath and just let your ribs and diaphragm go. Feel that outrush of air? There is no control in that release.

The controlled breath support is what we use for normal, easy breathing. We also use it for normal, conversational speech.

Controlled support is easy to do and easy to control. If you practice it, you can use it any time you need to, even when you are singing.

Power Breath Support

Now let's look at what the body naturally does when you need powerful breath support.

When you get something stuck in your throat, your body uses your breath to dislodge it. Your body drops into survival mode and automatically uses the most powerful and efficient method to force air out of your lungs. That is, you *cough*. To feel what your body does in this survival technique, do the following exercise.

1. Power Breath Support Exercise

Place your hands, thumbs toward the back, in the soft area between your ribs and your hips. Press in a little, so you are aware of your hands and your hands are aware of the muscles around your waist. These are your belt muscles. Do two gentle coughs. I emphasize "gentle," because hard coughing is not good for your voice. Do two gentle coughs and feel what happens under your hands. Did you feel a little outward bounce around your waist? Try it again. Two gentle coughs. Feel the outward bounce.

You could also do this exercise with a sneeze. But a sneeze is harder to do at will. However, the next time you sneeze, try to have the presence of mind to be aware of what your belt muscles are doing.

As you do the next exercise, don't let your ribs collapse. Keep them up and open. Shoulders down.

Now recreate that belt muscle bounce with two short "ss" breaths.

This way: 2 gentle coughs, 2 "sss" out flow of breaths. Make sure your belt muscles do the same bounce on the "sss" breaths that they do on the coughs. Repeat the exercise several times. Then repeat the exercise using "fff," instead of "sss."

Once you can recreate the belt muscle bounce, stop doing the coughs and just do 4 "s" or "f" breaths. Ready, Breathe, "f" "f" "f" "f." Let the old air out. Repeat the 4 "f" breath exercise several times.

A little explanation about the outward bounce. All that is happening is that your abdominal and lower back muscles are firming up. When a muscle firms up, it gets larger, or bulges, like your biceps. You might think that this outward bounce is opposite to what the body should do to expel air. You might think that to expel air you should squeeze in, like a tube of toothpaste. Seems logical, but that is not what the body does automatically. Your body does other things in this powerful exhalation, but there is no reason to complicate the exercise. If you can control the belt muscle bounce, you will have good breath support.

However, the belt muscle bounce will not allow you to speak or sing smoothly. You need to be able to support long, even tones. That means you need to be able to exhale your breath with a sustained, even flow with no bounce.

2. Power Breath Support Exercise

How does your body do that naturally? Have you ever blown up a balloon? Do this exercise. Place one hand in the soft area between your ribs and your hips. Press in a little, so you can feel your belt muscles. Pretend your other hand is a balloon that you are going to blow up through your thumb. Ready. Blow. Feel what is happening with your belt muscles. Did you feel them firming up? It feels like you are pushing out all the way around your belt area.

If you feel like you are pulling in with your belt muscles, try feeling as though you are resisting outward against your belt, all the way around - especially in the lower back. You will find that you have much more power and much more control.

The breath pressure you must exert to blow up a balloon is over - kill for creating sound, but the principle is the same.

3. Power Breath Support Exercise

As an exercise to gain control of this powerful support, place your hands against your belt muscles and blow out for four counts against an "s" breath. Ready, "ssss." Release. Do the exercise several times.

When you feel you have controlled support muscles under your control, start vocalizing with them.

This is such a powerful force, that you usually need far less effort than you think you need. When you want to sing louder and higher, use only as much effort as you need to easily create the sound you want. Don't tense up your abdomen. Abdominal tension can adversely affect the smooth flow of air and the operation of the rest of your body.

In singing, the air pressure is controlled to greater and lesser degrees throughout the song. We can apply these simple rules:

1. Higher tones receive more air pressure than lower tones.
2. Lower tones receive less air pressure than higher tones.
3. Louder tones receive more air pressure than softer tones.
4. Softer tones receive less air pressure than louder tones.

There needs to be a perfect balance between air pressure and vocal fold firmness for the control of range, dynamics and vibrato as we will soon discover.

Out and Down Support

The phrase "out and down support" is a good description of the physical sensations you feel when you use good breath support in singing. "Out and down support" gives you the most precise control of your breath pressure and breath flow, which is the basis of voice control. In "out and down support" you have a sense of keeping the ribs open and keeping the diaphragm down. Of course, as you gradually use up your air, the ribs come down and in and your diaphragm comes up, but you do not allow your ribs to collapse or your diaphragm to bounce back up.

As you have seen in the previous section, you control air pressure with the same muscles you use for laughing, coughing and sneezing. In "Great Singers on Great Singing," author, Metropolitan Opera Basso Jerome Hines, asks Metropolitan opera star Beverly Sills, "After you have begun to sing a phrase, do you constantly have the feeling of maintaining this outward expansion even though the ribs are continually moving in?" "Yes, sure," she replies. In the same book, Mr. Hines asks Luciano Pavarotti about support. "What sensation do you have when you take a breath before singing?" he asks. "The sensation is very simple. I don't know how you are going to describe this," he said in a discreet tone of voice, "but you take a breath and stay in the position as when you are in the bathroom... and you keep this position until the phrase is finished."

"In other words," Mr. Hines added, "you're basically working to keep the feeling down?"

"Because," he broke in, "*up* will come by itself. As the breath goes out, it comes up by itself, slowly, as you sing. . . as you speak. The great secret is to have the patience to let the diaphragm go down again before breathing the next phrase." "You mean," Mr. Hines said, "the bad tendency is to let the diaphragm stay up between phrases?" "The balloon is not full again," he said.

You need to be especially careful at the beginning of a phrase, right after you have taken a breath. It is common for singers to take a good breath, then to let too much of it out as they begin to sing. Make sure you resist with your ribs as you let the air out. Never feel rigid or tense. There is the tendency to collapse the rib cage down.

When Italians speak of the diaphragm and support, they use the word, "appoggio," from the verb "appoggiare" which means "to lean." *Out and down* support gives you the sense of *leaning* and allows you precise control of air pressure. This way of supporting also gives you access to power which must be used within appropriate limits in order to keep your voice healthy. Never send the air so hard that the tone loses its ring, intensity and beauty.

Singers Beware!

The number one killer of the voice is forcing too much air through the vocal folds, particularly on high and loud pitches. Your support muscles can create much greater breath pressure than your vocal folds can resist. Pushing too much air through the vocal folds dries them out and irritates them, resulting in a tired or hoarse voice, and losing beauty of tone.

Exercises

(Singing Techniques CD, Track 4)

1. Place your hands in the soft area between your hips and your ribs. Press in firmly. Now, cough gently 2 times. Feel the outward pulse around your abdomen. Feel it again, using a loud hiss (sss, sss). Now, on "F" as in *fame* (fff, fff). Make sure you feel the same gentle but firm outward pressure against your finger tips. Be sure to keep your lower ribs expanded.

(Singing Techniques CD, Track 5)

2. Now, feel your support working behind a vocal tone. Use 2 strong hisses followed by an easy, "shout-like" sound. Breathe (√) after the 2 hisses, before "Hey!":

   (√) sss, sss (√) hey!

   Feel the support just before the beginning of the vocal sound and continue to the end of the phrase. Feel the same easy out and down, firm, steady support on the shout- like sound "Hey!" as on the hisses.

3. Repeat three times.

   (√) sss, sss (√) hey!
   (√) sss, sss (√) hey!
   (√) sss, sss (√) hey!

4. Repeat with a longer tone at the end like this:

   (√) sss, sss (√) heeeeeeeeey!

5. Now repeat in the lower register of the female voice.

6. Men sing along.

7. Repeat in head voice, the upper register for the female voice and falsetto for the male voice, on the vowel:

   eeeeeeee (as in he)

8. Repeat three times in a row.

Additional Exercises

1. You can use this exercise first with hisses, then other open vowel sounds. Try it in various parts of your vocal range - low, middle and high, soft and loud.

   sss, sss (√) eeeeeeee (as in h<u>e</u>)
   sss, sss (√) aaaaaaaa (as in h<u>a</u>t)
   sss, sss (√) oooooooo (as in y<u>ou</u>)
   sss, sss (√) aaaaaaah (as in h<u>o</u>t)
   sss, sss (√) uuuuuuuh (as in h<u>u</u>m)
   sss, sss (√) aaaaaaaw (as in <u>aw</u>ning)
   etc.

   Whether we sing high or low notes at high or low volumes, the support must be kept steady, through to the end of the phrase.

2. To check your support, use your finger tips on your ribs, then use your thumbs against your lower back for steady resistance, and hiss:

   loud: s s s s s s s s
   (√) (support ——)
   soft: s s s s s s s s
   (√) (support ——)

3. Use the following exercise to practice "dynamics," that is, volume control. To gradually get louder (crescendo), we begin with a softer hiss and gradually increase our air pressure. To gradually get softer (decrescendo), we begin with a louder hiss and gradually decrease our air pressure without relaxing support. Use your finger tips to check.

   Crescendo:
   (√) (support ——) ⟨
   Decrescendo:
   (√) (support ——) ⟩

SING!

NOTES

CHAPTER THREE

Focusing the Vocal Folds

"Elisabeth Howard and I have shared workshops and conferences throughout the world... I have been fortunate to observe the popularity and effectiveness of her unique work. Her impressive versatility as a singer and her superb musicality are important factors in her successful work."

Marvin Keenze
Professor of Voice and Pedagogy,
The Westminster Choir College of Rider University
International Coordinator, National Assn. of Teachers of Singing

(Singing Techniques CD, Tracks 6-7)

A vocal sound that projects well is a sound that utilizes the air efficiently as air passes through vocal folds that are *approximating* or *adducting*. The vocal folds vibrate, producing a clear, "non breathy" vocal sound. In the Vocal Power method, we call this 'focusing' the vocal folds. Another term for vocal folds is *vocal cords*. Vocal folds has become more widely used among voice teachers and doctors. Look at the simplified drawings of the open and closed vocal folds in Figure A, below. The narrow end of the top view is the front of your larynx. It is just inside the bony structure you can feel at the front of your throat, often referred to as the "Adam's apple."

Vocal Folds (Cords)

Top View

Open Folds

Focused
(Closed) Folds

Front View

Open vocal folds
no vocal cord vibration
no vocal sound
breathing, whispering

Focused (Closed) Folds
vocal cord vibration
vocal sound

Figure A

When your vocal folds are open (*abducted*), you can breathe easily. The air (breath) passes in and out of your lungs with no obstruction.

When your vocal folds are closed (*approximated, adducted, focused*), they block the free flow of air (breath).

The action of the vocal folds when they vibrate is like this: the folds close, blocking the flow of air (breath) out of your lungs. You send the air with a little more air pressure (this is called support), which forces the vocal folds to open and release a little puff of air. This opening also releases the breath pressure, which allows the vocal folds to close again. Breath pressure once again builds up and forces the vocal folds apart, releasing a little puff of air. This action repeats itself over and over, as long as you keep the folds focused and maintain steady breath pressure. This vibration of the vocal folds creates vocal sound.

Glottal Attack

There are two ways of focusing your vocal folds. One is by forcing the folds together, as in a cough. This is called a *glottal attack*. The *glottis* is the slit between the vocal folds. Coughing and forceful glottal "attacks" are harmful to the vocal folds if done too hard and allowed to continue over long periods. If you allow air through the vocal folds, they open and this is called *abduction*, the opposite of closing the vocal folds which is *adduction*. (Air pressure below the glottis is called sub glottal air pressure.) However, we are going to show you some exercises that help train the vocal folds to approximate (close) correctly and develop their strength and stamina.

Bernoulli Effect

The other way of focusing your vocal folds is using a light touch called the *Bernoulli effect*. This is an amazing phenomenon that you can demonstrate for yourself. Hold a piece of paper (typing paper works well) by two corners along the short edge. Place the edge you are holding just below your lower lip and blow strongly across the top of the paper. Surprisingly, the paper, which was hanging down, rises and flaps as you blow across its top. The reason is that the fast moving air creates a partial vacuum across the top of the paper and the higher air pressure underneath the paper pushes the paper up into the vacuum. Another way of saying this is that the paper is drawn up into the partial vacuum. That is the *Bernoulli effect*. (As a point of interest, this is also the effect that keeps prop airplanes up in the air. Pretty powerful.)

How does this apply to focusing your vocal folds? In this way: when you bring your vocal folds close together and send (blow) air between them, the air goes faster through the narrow gap between the folds, creating a partial vacuum. The edges of the vocal folds are drawn together by this partial vacuum. This blocks off the flow of air, starting the vibration cycle. So, with the *Bernoulli effect,* instead of muscularly pushing the vocal folds together, as in a glottal attack, the vocal folds are drawn together lightly.

Both ways of focusing the vocal folds are used by good singers for different effects, as you will see in later chapters.

When unfocused, the vocal folds are too open, allowing too much air through, resulting in a breathy and sometimes raspy tone. This can cause friction and irritation of the vocal fold tissue. You may even feel a tickle which could cause you to cough. Blowing too much air past your vocal folds dries them out.

Prolonged breathy or raspy singing can cause the build-up of excessive mucus. This is the body's mechanism for protecting the vocal folds. Remember, when singing high and loud, don't push the air so hard that you unfocus your voice and produce a breathy or raspy sound. However, even though the folds must be focused for healthy singing, in some isolated moments breathiness or raspiness may be actually desirable for emotional emphasis.

Because more air must be used to produce the unfocused tones, it is more difficult to sing long, sustained phrases with unfocused vocal folds. This is why some singers are constantly out of breath. Breathy singing can be exhausting and can bring down the energy level of the performance.

Focusing your vocal folds helps you to sustain tones, reduces throat problems, because you are not trying to accomplish a clear tone by using extrinsic (outside) throat or neck muscles to help focus the tone. Focusing makes it easier for you to expand your range and improves your vocal flexibility. Focusing makes it easier to sing clear vowels.

Forward Placement
The "Mask"

Forward placement, or *mask* resonance, may be described as the vibrations generated by focused vocal folds that resonate in the hard surfaces of the nose, the upper front teeth, the forehead and cheek bone areas of the face. (see Chap. 7, *Good Vibrations! Vocal Colors: Resonance,* p. 55). This is the sound that we admire in professional singers that projects clearly and powerfully.

The following exercises will help you to gain control over focusing the vocal folds and develop mask resonance.

Exercises

(Singing Techniques CD, Track 6)

1. Open your mouth, take in a breath and let out a breathy sigh. This breathy sound is the result of allowing excessive air through the vocal folds which are too open. This is an unfocused tone.

2. With your mouth open, as if ready to bite an apple, in a gentle but firm scolding tone, say "aa ... aa ... aaaa" ("a" as in *hat*) [æ].
   Don't "cough" out the tone, make a clear non-breathy sound. Listen and feel the 'buzzing' sound of the focused tone. Feel your support and use your finger tips to make sure it stays constant.

3. Once more compare the unfocused tone with the clear, well focused tone:

   (sigh, breathy) aa ... aa ... aaa
   (clear, focused) aa ... aa ... aaa

4. Now sustain the last "aa," like this:

   (focused) aa ... aa ... aaaaaaaaaaaa

   Maintain an energetic and buzzing sound as you sustain the vowel. Breathiness is an appropriate artistic choice at times but should be used sparingly and avoided completely in the high and loud ranges of the voice.

5. Now follow the "aa" sound with the "ee" sound. Try to match the buzzing, focused sound that you feel on "aa," like this:

   aa ... aa ... eeeeeeee (as in h<u>e</u>)

(Singing Techniques CD, Track 7)

6. Let's carry the focused tone into some other vowels. The symbols in brackets are from the International Phonetic Alphabet (IPA), which makes it easier, through sound symbols to learn the sounds in almost any language throughout the world.

For example:

aa ... aa ... eh [ε]   (as in h<u>e</u>n)

aa ... aa ... ah [ɑ]   (as in h<u>o</u>t)

aa ... aa ... uh [ʌ]   (as in l<u>o</u>ve)

aa ... aa ... aw [ɔ]   (as in d<u>aw</u>n)

aa ... aa ... uh [ʊ]   (as in b<u>oo</u>k)

Be sure that the vowel that follows the "aa" [æ] vowel does not become unfocused or breathy.

Continue with this exercise, using the vowel sounds in the list on p. 17 and 18.

Helpful Hints

1. Prepare your intake of air by *thinking low* into the lower back while expanding your ribs and lower abdomen.
2. Prepare your support just prior to the sound.
3. Imagine the beautiful and focused sound you want to hear just prior to the sound.

Special Note

4. If you are having trouble resonating your [ɑ] as in f<u>ar</u>, [ɔ] as in d<u>aw</u>n, [ʊ] as in b<u>oo</u>k, or [u] as in s<u>oo</u>n: Think of your tongue *toward* the vowel sound [i] as in s<u>ee</u>. That is, slightly raised in the middle toward the front upper molars. There is a tendency to pull the tongue down in the back to "make space" for the tone. But pressing the tongue down in the back causes tension or pressure that can damp the vocal folds and inhibit their vibrations. Tongue tension can also alter the pitch of the tone. If you find you are singing flat, use the tongue release exercise on pages 52 and 53.

Benefits

With focused vocal folds and air pressure in balance, you will experience:
1. Tones that can be described as *ringing, buzzing*, having a *core,* an *edge*.
2. Tones that project efficiently without excess air.
3. Singing longer phrases with the least amount of effort.
4. Stronger vocal folds that will last for longer periods of time.

CHAPTER FOUR

Articulation

"Elisabeth Howard's Vocal Power Method is so comprehensive that you will receive more in one sitting than you will with most teachers in a year's worth of instruction."

Laurie Lee Cosby
Director, Studio Bella Voice; Vocal Power Associate, Houston, TX

(Singing Techniques CD, Tracks 8-12)

*"There are two unbreakable rules of good speech:
1) You must be heard. 2) You must be understood."*

This is a quote from American Diction for Singers," by Geoffrey G. Forward. We have already learned in the previous chapters how to project a tone through breathing, support and focusing our vocal folds. Being understood has to do with the way we pronounce our words.

Pronunciation involves how we say vowels, consonants and dipthongs that make up words. For example, whether you say "wire" for the words, "why are," or "a pie," for the words, "up high," makes a big difference in your being understood by your audience.

Articulation involves the movement of your articulators and the positions you put them in to sing these words. Your articulators are your lips, teeth, tongue, hard palate and soft palate. Articulation also involves *linking,* which is connecting words for a free flow of singing. Linking is also referred to as *liaison*, a French word meaning "joining, bonding."

Vowels

Words are made up of vowels and consonants. The articulation of these sounds is what projects the meanings of the words. Vowel sounds are the open sounds on tones that singers sustain (hold). Vowel sounds for singing are not the same as we were taught in school: A-E-I-O-U. If that were so, how would you pronounce "book?" Would you pronounce the "oo" in "book" like the "oo" in "soon?" No, of course not.

In English, we can not depend on the *spelling* of the word for its pronunciation. The word, "see," has the same vowel sound as the word, "sea." These two vowel sounds are pronounced exactly the same [i], but are spelled differently and have different meanings. We must have a very clear idea what vowel sound we are going to sustain in order to be understood.

Note: The clearer you pronounce your vowel, the better the focus of your vocal folds will be, thus better projection of not only the resonance, but the meaning of the word.

Hard and Soft Palate

You can locate your *hard palate* by touching your tongue to the roof of your mouth. It cannot be moved. By moving your tongue closer or further from your hard palate you can create different sounds. If you touch your tongue a little farther back in the roof of your mouth

SING!

you come to a soft and flexible area. This is your *soft palate*, a muscle that can open up or close the throat passage into the nasal area.

Tongue Vowels

The tongue should be flexible and move freely for the correct articulation of words. The tongue should not tense and press down in the back of the throat. This un-wanted tongue tension or pressure can dampen the vibrations of the vocal folds, thus interfering with the focusing of the vocal folds, affecting projection of the sound and can also *flat* the pitch. To sustain a vowel sound, the tip of the tongue rests behind the lower teeth and moves only to articulate consonants and quickly returns to its resting place behind the lower teeth for the vowels.

In the following progression below, the tongue begins in an arched position with the tip resting against the lower teeth and the sides of the tongue raised up on either side against the molars toward the front of the mouth. It gradually lowers from its highest position for "ee" [i] (as in s<u>ee</u>) to its lowest position for "uh" [ʌ] (as in <u>u</u>p).

	I.P.A.*
"ee" as in s<u>ee</u>	[i]
"ih" as in s<u>i</u>t	[ɪ]
"eh" as in wh<u>e</u>n	[ɛ]
"aa" as in th<u>a</u>t	[æ]
"a" as in p<u>a</u>rk	[a]**
"ah" as in f<u>a</u>r	[ɑ]
"uh" as in l<u>o</u>ve	[ʌ]
"aw" as in d<u>a</u>wn	[ɔ]
"uu" it as in b<u>oo</u>k	[ʊ]
"oo" as in y<u>ou</u>	[u]

*I.P.A.: International Phonetic Alphabet

** "a" as in the bright Boston vowel "Park the Car" would be *Paaahk the caaah.*

Lip Vowels

Lip vowels involve the shaping of the lips more forward to sound the correct vowel. The lips are involved in [ɔ] (as in d<u>a</u>wn) [ʊ] (as in b<u>oo</u>k) and [u] (as in s<u>oo</u>n). The lips form a rounded and slightly forward position as in drinking from a straw for these vowel sounds, and are most rounded for [u]. The tip of the tongue rests behind the lower teeth for all the vowels.

The mouth, widened toward an "inner smile," not a grimace, helps to activate the mask resonance (see page 58), adding overtones that give the voice resonance throughout its range. Let your eye teeth show slightly on your highest notes, but be careful not to wrinkle your nose or tense your lips unnaturally.

On lower notes there is a tendency to lose focus because the vocal folds are looser. Mask placement helps to focus the vocal folds. When you are singing on a low pitch, you can brighten your vowel sound and achieve a clearer sound by slightly widening your mouth position toward a smile. This helps to emphasize the upper resonances and maintain the mask placement.

If the expression of a word indicates sorrow, your eyes communicate the emotion and your mouth can still widen slightly, especially on higher and/or louder tones. Notice that in both crying and smiling the expression of the mouth is similar.

[i] and [u]

For the vowels: [i] (as in s<u>ee</u>), [ɪ] (as in s<u>i</u>t) and [u] (as in s<u>oon</u>), there is a tendency to close the jaw for these sounds. Keep a finger width or more between your teeth for your low notes and to make space for your higher notes. The jaw should not move the tongue up to say these vowels. The tongue must be independent of the jaw for correct articulation and for a more open sound, consistent with the other vowels in the phrase.

The tongue creates the "ee" [i] sound. The sides of the tongue lightly touch the upper molars and the tip rests behind the lower teeth. High notes and loud notes need more resonating space to sound free and easy. Because of the more open space, the vowels become slightly modified. When the "ee" [i] (as in s<u>ee</u>) vowel occurs on a high note, it is best to move the tongue slightly toward the "ih" [ɪ] (as in s<u>i</u>t) vowel and open the jaw a little more in order to produce a free and open vowel sound. At the same time you should try to keep the "ee" [i] vowel as pure as possible. This approach applies to especially to louder tones throughout the range, especially if the chest color is emphasized (for resonance, see page 55).

The lips form the "oo" [u] (as in s<u>oon</u>) sound by moving forward and rounding while the tongue remains relaxed. For both high notes and louder tones, relax the jaw more open than when you say "oo" in the speaking range. But even when the jaw is more open, try to keep a true "oo" vowel by rounding the lips around the mouth. When you round your lips, be careful not to protrude them too forward in an unbecoming manner. I would venture to say however, that basses and baritones when singing in a more classical style, will use more forward positions of the lips for more depth of tone.

Exercise

1. Open your mouth about an inch and a half, that's about two finger widths, and touch your finger tips against your chin to help your jaw stay open and say:
   ah ... ah (as in f<u>a</u>r) ... ee...ee [i] (as in s<u>ee</u>) .
   Notice the tendency to close the jaw on the "ee" vowel.
   Now, do it again, keeping the open space you feel on the "ah" vowel right through the "ee" vowel. Say the "ee" with the tip of the tongue resting against the backs of the lower front teeth.
   Repeat the exercise for both the "ih" and the "oo" vowels.
   ah ... ah ... iiiiiih [ɪ] (as in <u>i</u>t).
   ah ... ah ... ooooooo [u] (as in s<u>oon</u>).

The following exercises will be helpful in developing a clear and well projected tone in the upper register (head voice), which is falsetto for the male voice. It will also help develop the lower register (chest voice).

As we will discover, the upper register can be used as an upward extension of the chest voice which we call the "*mix*" or "*belt mix*" (see Chap.9, *The Pop Sound: Belt Mix*, p. 67).

Use these exercises to strengthen your upper register. "ee" is a good practice vowel for this purpose.

Exercises

(Singing Techniques CD, Track 8)

1. On a siren-like "ee" [i] sound, try this:

   ee ... ee ... eeeeeeeeeeeeeeeeeeeeeeee
   slide up   slide down

SING!

2. Now follow the "ee" vowel with other vowel sounds beginning with "eh" (as in end), [ɛ] like this:

   ee ... ee ... eeeh [ɛ] (as in h<u>e</u>n)

   ee ... ee ... eeah [ɑ] (as in h<u>o</u>t)

   ee ... ee ... eeuh [ʌ] (as in l<u>o</u>ve)

   ee ... ee ... eeaw [ɔ] (as in d<u>aw</u>n)

   ee ... ee ... eeuuh [ʊ] (as in b<u>oo</u>k)

   ee ... ee ... eeoo [u] (as in y<u>ou</u>)

(Singing Techniques CD, Track 9)

3. Now, using what we know about breath, support, focusing and open space, make the scale part of the following exercise as smooth as the slide that precedes it.

   Sing: "aa" [æ] (as in <u>a</u>t)

4. Repeat the above exercise, using "aa" [æ] on the slide and the following vowel sounds on the scale. Be sure that you keep the focus and the forward placement that you feel on the "aa" vowel in the vowel that follows it.

   (slide) aaaa ... (scale) aaaaaah [ɑ] (as in h<u>o</u>t)
   (slide) aaaa ... (scale) uuuuuh [ʌ] (as in l<u>o</u>ve)
   (slide) aaaa ... (scale) aaaaaaw [ɔ] (as in d<u>aw</u>n)
   (slide) aaaa ... (scale) uuuuuh [ʊ] (as in b<u>oo</u>k)
   (slide) aaaa ... (scale) oooooo [u] (as in y<u>ou</u>)
   (slide) aaaa ... (scale) eeeeeeh [ɛ] (as in h<u>e</u>n)
   (slide) aaaa ... (scale) eeeeeee [i] (as in h<u>e</u>)

(Singing Techniques CD, Track 10)

5. Now try it in the head voice range.

   Sing:

6. Beginning one half step higher each time, follow the "ee" [i] vowel with "oo" [u] (as in s<u>oo</u>n) then "aw" [ɔ] (as in d<u>aw</u>n) and "ah" [ɑ] (as in f<u>a</u>r) and work through this list.

Diphthongs

A diphthong is a combination vowel, actually two vowel sounds, one immediately following one after the other. For singing, the I.P.A. Symbol used here reflects vowel sounds that are slightly modified from those used in speech.

	I.P.A.
My ... (M/ah/ih)	[ɑɪ]
[ɑ] (as in f<u>a</u>r) [ɪ] (as in <u>i</u>t)	
Day ... (D/eh/ih)	[ɛɪ]
[ɛ] (as in <u>e</u>nd) [ɪ] (as in <u>i</u>t)	
Boy ... (B/aw/ih)	[ɔɪ]
[ɔ] (as in d<u>aw</u>n) [ɪ] (as in <u>i</u>t)	
Now ... (N/ɑ/ʊ)	[ɑʊ]
[ɑ] (as in f<u>a</u>r) [ʊ] (as in b<u>oo</u>k)	
Go ... (G/ɔ/ʊ)	[ɔʊ]
[ɔ] (as in dawn) [ʊ] (as in b<u>oo</u>k)	

For singing, "y" is pronounced [I] (as in <u>i</u>t). For example: "you" is pronounced [Iu]. "W" is pronounced as [u] (as in s<u>oo</u>n). For example: "want" is pronounced u/a/nt.

In non-classical style, the voiceless "wh" sound, as in the words, "where," "when," "what" and "why," I use the voiced "w" (oo) [u], rather than the breathy "Wh." In classical singing, it is correct for the "wh" to begin with the breathy sound as if blowing out a candle.

Depending on the style of music, the second vowel sound of the dipthong may be exaggerated. For example, in country western style, the word "day" may be sung like this: *deiii.* You can also soften the [i] sound at the end of the word by pronouncing [I] (as in <u>i</u>t) instead of [i] (as in see). For example: "day" [ɛɪ]. You may choose to soften the [u] sound in "Go" G/ɔ/u by pronouncing it [ʊ] (as in b<u>oo</u>k) instead of [u] (as in s<u>oo</u>n) G/ɔʊ. It really depends on the style of vocal music you are singing, as well as your personal style. Some singers have become well known for their unusual pronunciation.

(Singing Techniques CD, Track 11)

Consonants

Consonant sounds are also formed by movement of the articulators. They help make words clear, give expression to the word and help project the sound. But if you don't articulate them properly they can interfere with the focus of the vocal folds and block the free flow of sound.

Voiced and Voiceless Consonants

The voiced consonants are those in which the vocal folds vibrate, creating vocal sound. Place your finger tips at the front of your throat and say, "*ssss*" (as in *sue*), with a good, strong hissing sound. Notice there is no vibration against your finger tips. Voiceless consonants are those in which the vocal folds are open and do not vibrate.

Say "*zzzz*" (as in *zoo*), with a strong buzzing sound. That vibration you feel against your finger tips is from your vibrating vocal folds. The voiced consonant requires the vocal folds to focus and vibrate.

Voiceless consonants create a gap in the stream of vocal tone by requiring the vocal folds to part. With your finger tips at your throat, say "*the zoo*" and then say "*with Sue.*" Notice the interruption of vibration during the "*ssss*" in "*Sue.*" The vocal folds do not focus on voiceless consonants.

Because the vocal folds are open for the voiceless consonants, they have a tendency to stay partially open during the vowel that follows. This creates an undesirable breathiness and loss of projection or can even cause the voice to "crack" from a focused tone, to no tone at all.

Silent H

"H" is an unvoiced consonant that does not require the action of the articulators. The "Silent H" is useful in avoiding a glottal attack on a word beginning with a vowel. (see page 41).

Below are pairs of voiced and voiceless consonants. The position of the articulators are approximately in the same position for each pair. Notice the IPA symbols for the consonants.

Exercises

	[Voiced]	[Voiceless]

Articulate with the lips.

b (as in *bay*) p (as in *pay*)	[b]	[p]

Articulate with the front of the tongue and upper gum ridge, just behind the upper front teeth.

d (as in *do*) t (as in *too*)	[d]	[t]

Articulate with the back of the tongue and soft palate.

g (as in *glue*) k (as in *clue*)	[g]	[k]

Articulate with the front of the tongue and gum ridge.

g (as in *gem*) ch (as in *chat*)	[dʒ]	[tʃ]

Articulate with the front of the tongue and teeth.

th (as in *the*) th (as in *thanks*)	[ð]	[θ]

Articulate with the upper teeth and lower lip.

v (as in *van*) f (as in *fan*)	[v]	[f]

Articulate with the tongue and teeth.

z (as in *zoo*) s (as in *Sue*)	[z]	[s]
s (as in *treasure*) s (as *insure*)	[ʒ]	[ʃ]

Helpful Hints

1. When singing a voiceless consonant, immediately focus the vowel that follows the voiceless consonant. Think the focused vowel even before you pronounce the consonant.
2. Sing on the pure vowel sound and don't rush to the next consonant.

Other Voiced Consonants

l (as in *line*)	[l]
m (as in *more*)	[m]
n (as in *now*)	[n]
ng (as in *long*)	[ŋ]
r (as in *reel*)	[r]

Consonants may also appear in combination. For example:

bz (as in *grabs*)	[bz]
ps (as in *laps*)	[ps]
dz (as in *goods*)	[dz]
ts (as in *pats*)	[ts]
gz (as in *dogs*)	[gz]
ks (as in *socks*)	[ks]

Note: Following a voiced consonant, the "s" is pronounced "z" as in *grabs, goods* and *dogs.* Following a voiceless consonant the "s" is pronounced "s" as in *laps, pats* and *socks.*

Exercises:

(Singing Techniques CD, Track 12)

1. Make the vowel in the word as well focused as the two that precede it.
Sing:

2. Practice both the chest voice and head voice (falsetto for males).
Sing:

eh	*eh*	*ten*	[ɛ]
ee	*ee*	*key*	[i]
uh	*uh*	*fun*	[ʌ]
oh	*oh*	*stone*	[ɔu]
ah	*ah*	*heart*	[a]
oo	*oo*	*school*	[u]

3. You can feel the vocal folds alternately focus and unfocus in the following exercise. Both consonants in each pair require the same position of the articulators. But the voiceless consonants "s" and "f" require the vocal folds to be unfocused. Keep a steady flow of air as you alternate between "zzzzzzz" (voiced) and "sssssss" (voiceless), and "vvvvvvv" and "fffff".

(√) zzzzzsssssszzzzzzssssszzzzzssss and:

(√) vvvvvfffffvvvvvfffffvvvvvfffff

4. In the following exercise, match the focus of "aa" (as in *at*) [æ] in the vowel of the word that follows it. Don't let the voiceless consonant introduce excessive breath into the vocal tone.

aaa ... aaa ... *saaat*
aaa ... aaa ... *maaad*
aaa ... aaa ... *paaatch*
aaa ... aaa ... *scaaan*
aaa ... aaa ... *chaaance*
aaa ... aaa ... *faaan*
aaa ... aaa ... *shaaall*
aaa ... aaa ... *staaand*

5. Using the following pairs of voiced and voiceless consonants, speak, then sing, on a single note.

do	too	do	too	[u]
bay	pay	bay	pay	[ɛ¹]
glue	clue	glue	clue	[u]
junk	chunk	junk	chunk	[ʌ]
the	thud	the	thud	[ʌ]
van	fan	van	fan	[æ]
zoo	Sue	zoo	Sue	[u]

6. In the following exercise, focus the vowel immediately. Do not allow the voiceless consonant to introduce excessive breath into the vocal tone. Use "aa" [æ] (as in *at*) On a single note,
Sing:

aa	ee	[i]	seem
aa	ih	[ɪ]	fill
aa	eh	[ɛ]	tend
aa	aa	[æ]	pal
aa	aa	[æ]	tab
aa	uh	[ʌ]	thunder
aa	aw	[ɔ]	fought
aa	uu	[ʊ]	could
aa	oo	[u]	you

CHAPTER FIVE

Dynamics

"The Vocal Power Method is fun and easy to learn... and has been so helpful when preparing for auditions."

Kelly Packard
"Bay Watch," "Ripley's Believe It or Not," "California Dreams"

(Singing Techniques CD, Tracks 13-15)

To be truly free and expressive in your singing, you must be able to sing a variety of volume levels. When we speak, we naturally emphasis the important words. Some words are louder and some are softer, otherwise we would speak with the same volume level throughout our speech. This would be boring. We don't think about it as we speak with feelings and emotions. It should be the same when we sing. What is different in singing? In singing, we sustain words longer than we do in speech. Sometimes we increase the volume level in a phrase or on a single, sustained tone (crescendo), or decrease (decrescendo) the volume level in a phrase or on a single, sustained tone. This means that our vocal skills need to be automatic, since they serve our emotions.

To sing with greater volume (*forte, f*), we use more air pressure and more vocal fold focusing strength at the same time. When the interaction between the air pressure and the vocal folds is perfectly balanced, you will experience a "buzz" or "ring" in your tone. You can add more volume by using more chest color and mask resonance along with more vocal fold focusing strength and more air pressure. Be careful not to overpower your vocal folds with too much air pressure (see *Good Vibrations! Vocal Colors: Placement*, page 55). Forcing air pressure too much against your vocal folds will stop the free vibrations of the folds and will cause strain and hoarseness. You should never feel pain or strain when you sing. Even the most powerful and projected tones should have a sense of ease. If everything is in balance - vocal folds - air pressure and resonance - you will feel this effortless sensation in your singing and have dependability and longevity.

To sing with softer volume (*piano, p*), we use less air pressure and less vocal fold focusing strength at the same time. You can use any of the four colors or resonances for piano singing (see *Good Vibrations! Vocal Colors: Placement*, page 55). When the interaction between the air pressure and the vocal folds is perfectly balanced, you will experience a clear, yet soft tone. If the tone gets breathy, use less air. For the softest tones, only the delicate fringes of the vocal folds vibrate. To help relax the vocal folds for softer tones, lift the soft palate with a yawn-like sensation. Make sure that in lifting the soft palate, the tongue stays forward in the correct position for the vowel and not pulled back in the throat as we do in a real yawn. Be careful to maintain firm, steady, out and down support throughout.

Note: Extraneous air through the vocal folds creates breathiness or a raspy sound which in some instances is desirable, for example in soft, breathy, intimate songs or loud agressive music where a raspy sound might be more appropriate. Be aware that high, loud and breathy tones can be damaging to the voice.

Exercises

(Singing Techniques CD, Track 13)

1. Higher chest voices sing on a not too loud shout-like, sound. Let it drop off in pitch at the end.
   Sing:

2. Follow this shout-like sound with a "far-away shout" or "echo" of the shout.
   Sing:

3. Try this exercise, first in lower register and then an octave higher in upper register.
   Sing:

4. Use the word "Hello," first loud, then "far-away."
   Sing:

5. Now, in head voice. First loud, then "far-away."
   Sing:

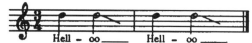

Crescendo and Decrescendo

(Singing Techniques CD, Track 14)

To crescendo (———————————), which is beginning soft and gradually becoming louder, begin with a soft tone and gradually increase the vocal fold focusing strength and air pressure at the same time. Feel the yawn and maintain firm support. For maximum volume, make sure the mask and chest colors are utilized to their fullest extent. (See Chapter 7, *Good Vibrations! Vocal Colors Resonance*, page 55).

To decrescendo (———————————), which is beginning loud and gradually becoming softer, begin with a louder tone and gradually decrease focusing strength and air pressure at the same time. Maintain steady support from the beginning to the end.

Note: It is possible to use less air pressure and still support for the softer tones. You can test this out by taking a breath, prepare your support muscles as if you were about to sing and don't sing. No sound is being heard at all, yet you are still feeling support.

Although the vocal folds relax for softer volume, they must still produce a clear tone throughout and the vowel must be kept pure. When singing softer, you will still hear resonance because your vocal folds are still vibrating and focusing, but you won't hear an *edge* or *buzz* in the sound. The soft tone will still project very well as long as the tone is resonant and not breathy.

Exercises

1. On a siren-like slide, first loud, then soft,
   Sing:

On the upward part of the slide, gradually increase air pressure and lower the jaw. On the downward part of the slide, decrease air pressure, bringing the jaw back to its normal position. Make sure you maintain your support on the downward slide. Check with your finger tips at your ribs and then with your thumbs against your lower back. Be aware of your focused vocal folds to maintain a clear sound throughout.

2. And now in upper register, first loud, then soft,
   Sing:

3. On the word "Hey," use the siren-like slide, followed by a 5 note scale within a comfortable vocal range and slide your voice slowly up and down with medium volume. Keep the volume and vowel constant throughout. Maintain the vocal folds in the focused position for a clear tone.
   Sing:

(Singing Techniques CD, Track 15)

4. Use the following 5 note scale with the words "on and on." First louder, then softer in the lower chest range (an octave higher for the female voice).
   Sing:

And in the higher chest voice range.
Sing:

5. And in head voice or falsetto, first louder, then softer.
Sing:

6. Let's sing that exercise loud to medium, to soft (decrescendo), using "Day by Day."
Sing:

7. Now decrescendo using your head voice (falsetto for men).
Sing:

8. Use the above exercises and practice your crescendo, beginning softly and gradually increasing to greater volume. Give your entire range a good workout by beginning in a low, comfortable range and working your way up into the higher range.

Note: If you are experiencing continual hoarseness, loss of the high range or a double tone on a particular note or notes, my advice is to check your vocal folds with a good laryngologist, one preferably that works with singers. Develop your range gradually. Singing too high or too low, especially for long periods of time can tire your voice, cause a raspy sound or even a double tone. Rest your voice and practice in moderation, a half hour at a time in the beginning. Increase your practice time as your voice feels stronger. The vocal instrument cannot be replaced. It has its limitations. Muscles get tired with over use and we are using our vocal folds and support muscles. Our concentration also has its limitations. Be careful and wise.

"Onset" " the Silent H "
Beginning the tone

There is a tendency to use a *glottal attack*, when singing a word that begins with a vowel. The glottal attack is holding the vocal folds closed and releasing them suddenly to begin the tone, like we do when we cough. Unless the desired effect is an emphasis on a particular word, using a glottal attack is not desirable. Also, too many glottal attacks disturb the smooth (legato) line of the phrase. A slight, inaudible "H" before a vowel at the beginning of a word will help prevent an audible glottal attack. At the beginning or "onset" of the word, the vocal folds should draw together in order to create a free sound and not "pop" open as in a cough. The "Silent H" is silent. Don't let your audience hear it. Lift the soft palate for an inaudible "Silent H."

Note: The "Silent H" works very well for both louder tones and also for the softest tones for beginning a tone on a vowel without a glottal attack.

Use the "Silent H" on a single note on the following words, ,
Sing:

I,   any,   at,   easy,   every,   air,
   each,   oh,   only,   over,   all, .   its,   I'm.

The BIG Voice Versus
The Small Voice

The inherent size of the voice is a much more significant factor in the performance of opera than in the performing of non-classical music. In opera or classical singing in general (recitals, oratorios, etc.), the voice is not typically amplified, except perhaps for out door performances. In commercial/pop music, the sound is almost always amplified. In music theater, it depends on the size of the venue, but even at high school productions, the lead voices are often electronically amplified.

In classical recitals, chamber music and oratorio, vocal size is not as important as beauty of tone, vocal skills, artistry and interpretation. There are singers, however, that are able to perform in all areas of classical music, from recitals to opera. Some singers, because of their lighter voices, specialize in the lighter operas of Mozart, Rossini, Bellini and Donizetti, as well as operettas and music theater, as compared to the more dramatic voices that sing roles in the operas of Puccini, Verdi and Wagner. Vocal quality and size of the vocal instrument may be more suited to a particular operatic style and it is important for the classical singer to find his or her "fach," a German word used to denote the category of voice type in opera. These voice types are most suited to certain roles and specialize in these roles.

A young singer would be wise to rely on the professional guidance of a voice teacher in choosing the correct repertoire as his or her voice develops and matures. Singing roles that are too heavy and beyond the vocal capabilities and endurance of one's vocal instrument too early in one's career, is not conducive to a long lasting career. In non-classical, commercial/pop singing styles from blues to jazz to rock, the emphasis is placed on personal style, sound, expression, *charisma* (stage presence) and image.

Note: In recordings, **BIG** or **small** voice, you can capture the hearts of your listening audience with the sound of your voice alone. Your vocal technique, through a variety of dynamics, vibrato and vocal colors are all at your command to help you express your emotions in interpreting the words. Consistent study and practice will bring great benefits to you for a long lasting career, no matter how big or small your voice.

No voice is too small for a professional career!

CHAPTER SIX

Vibrato

"Liz gave me my classical technique. I will never lose the bond that I have with her as a mentor, a teacher and a friend. Liz has astounding capabilities as a musician and technician of the vocal instrument."

Devon Guthrie
First Place, Los Angeles Music Center Spotlight Award
Student, Manhattan School of Music

(Singing Techniques CD, Tracks 16-20)

The control of vibrato is seldom explored in the study or teaching of voice, although it is one of the primary objectives in the study of stringed instruments and most wind instruments. Vibrato has always been somewhat of a mystery in the study of voice, since there are so many variations from singer to singer and from style to style. It can be confusing.

What is vibrato?

According to Webster's Dictionary, vibrato is "a pulsating effect produced by rapid alternation of a given tone." According to the New Grove Dictionary of Opera, "(It., from Lat. *vibrare*: to 'shake') A regular fluctuation of pitch and/or intensity, either more or less pronounced and either more or less rapid."

Vibrato for the singer is steady, even pulsations with a slight fluctuation of pitch and volume on a sustained tone. The average vibrato rate is 5 to 9 pulses per second. In general, the pitch variation should be minimized to an interval spanning about a quarter step. (A quarter step is half the span of a half-step interval.) If the pitch fluctuates an interval of a 3rd or more, it is considered a "wobble," not a desirable sound in singing.

For string instruments, vibrato is created by the fluctuation in pitch and not volume. A string player, such as a violinist or guitarist, creates the vibrato by pressing down on the string with the finger in a rapid back and forth motion. This motion causes the string to lengthen and shorten alternately, producing a slight fluctuation in pitch, thus achieving vibrato. A quicker back and forth motion produces a faster vibrato. A slower motion produces a slower vibrato. In wind instruments and voice, vibrato is achieved by both fluctuation in pitch and volume.

A wind player, such as a flautist or clarinetist produces vibrato by fluctuating the air pressure, sending it through the instrument in a pulsing, wave-like motion. On the pulse, the tone is louder. Between pulses, the tone is slightly softer, but because it is smooth, it is imperceptible to the audience. Vibrato may be controlled with the lips, throat and/or abdominal muscles and varies from player to player.

The choice concerning where to use the vibrato, and the speed of vibrato, is entirely up to the performer, instrumentalist and singer alike. It is a matter of taste.

Vibrato is a Tool of Expression

(Singing Techniques CD, Track 16)

Vibrato is a *tool of expression*. Vibrato not only enhances the sustained tone, but can be used as a means of expressing the various emotions associated with a word or phrase. As we study vibrato, we begin to notice the variations of vibrato types associated with musical styles: rhythm & blues, country western, opera, rock, etc. Show music from the Broadway stage ranges from operatic to rock style and can not be put in a category by itself anymore. The differences in the way vibrato is used in various styles will become more apparent the more we listen and analyze. This chapter on vibrato will help you to understand vibrato and make it clear to you how you can make choices in your own singing.

If your career is to include studio work, back-up or singing in a small ensemble or singing in a chorus, the ability to control your vibrato and *straight* tone with no vibrato, is a basic requirement. Vibrato control is crucial in the recording studio where you might need to sing with a straight tone, or a straight tone gradually moving into vibrato, or a faster vibrato, or a slower vibrato, or a vibrato that speeds up, or a vibrato with crescendo (gradually louder) or decrescendo (gradually softer), or you might need to *synchronize* your vibrato with other singers in a group.

Since vibrato has so many variations in fluctuation of pitch, volume and speed, a homogeneous sound among a group of singers using vibrato would be next to impossible. This is why vibrato is used sparingly in most choral singing, since blending is so important and vibrato varies from singer to singer. However, if you are a soloist singing with a chorus, and depending on the musical style, you would probably be expected to sing with a vibrato, but when you sing with the group, you must be able to use a straight tone with no vibrato, if required.

It all depends on the style of music and direction from your choral director. If you are singing in an opera chorus, vibrato is usually expected.

Isn't vibrato natural?

No one is born on the operating table with a vibrato. It isn't *natural*. Many singers say they have a natural vibrato, but it still is learned, whether by imitation of other singers or by the guidance from a voice teacher or both. Just think, if we were born on a desert island, with no music from the outside world, would we have a *natural* vibrato? You can only sing what you can hear. Vibrato varies from style to style of music and from culture to culture.

There are four types of vocal vibrato:
1. "Vocal Fold Flutter Vibrato"
2. "Throat Vibrato"
3. "Shimmering Vibrato"
4. "Diaphragmatic (Abdominal), on the Breath Vibrato"

Vocal Fold Flutter Vibrato

The *vocal fold flutter vibrato* is achieved by producing rapid interruptions, or a "flutter" in the focus of the vocal folds, as in a rapid laugh. The vocal fold flutter vibrato is typical of the singing styles of the French Chanteuse or Cabaret singer. The French legend, Edith Piaf, is an example of a singer who uses vocal fold flutter almost exclusively in her singing. For example, listen to her signature song, "La Vie en Rose." The French Canadian Pop star, Celine Dion, grew up singing French popular songs and often uses vocal fold flutter in some of her singing. As an example, listen to the song, "My Heart Will Go On," from the movie "Titanic."

You can hear vocal fold flutter vibrato in early twentieth century operetta style, particularly in the soprano voices, for example, the singing of Jeanette McDonald. It was also common in the style of American folk singers of the 1960's, for example in the singing of Joan Baez, Judy Collins and Buffy St. Marie.

Others who use vocal fold flutter: Jazz singer Nina Simone, Country Western singer Dolly Parton, International singer Julio Iglesias and 1960's novelty singer Tiny Tim.

Throat Vibrato

The *throat vibrato* is produced by pulsating the muscles of the pharyngeal wall in the rhythm of the vibrato, which creates fluctuations in pitch, but not necessarily in volume. This is not scientifically proved yet, more research needs to be done. Throat vibrato may be rapid and narrow in fluctuation of pitch, or slow and wide. It is heard in almost every musical style, but most typically in the pop genre. Singers like Dean Martin, Frank Sinatra and Elvis Presley use this type of vibrato in much of their singing. You will often hear jazz and blues singers use throat vibrato in a similar way to that used in jazz instrumental style. Many singers use both throat vibrato and diaphragmatic vibrato, sometimes in combination, sometimes one more than the other. You will not hear much throat vibrato alone in classical singing. The vibrato is mostly diaphragmatically based. Shimmering vibrato is used for faster passing notes that do not sustain.

Even though many singers use throat vibrato successfully, one needs to be aware that with throat vibrato, there is muscular activity which may or may not involve the root of the tongue. Too much tongue tension can flat the pitch. If you are having trouble staying on pitch, it may be simply that you are using too much tongue, jaw or throat tension to create throat vibrato.

Test for flatting:

1. Choose a comfortable pitch and sustain a straight tone with no vibrato.
2. Press in lightly with your finger just above your "Adam's Apple."

The pitch will flat. Diaphragmatic vibrato together with the *Tongue Release* exercise at the end of this chapter, will alleviate this unnecessary muscular tension, freeing the tone, but will still allow you to use some throat vibrato successfully for style.

Shimmering Vibrato

The *shimmering vibrato* is a very fast throat vibrato, heard in faster tempo songs, including classical style. Shimmering vibrato is typical in jazz "scat singing." The sensation is that the vocal folds themselves are pulsating. The more adduction of the vocal folds, the easier the shimmer.

The Continuing "Vibrato" Controversy

Note: Among professional voice teachers, singers, etc., there is still some controversy as to whether or not vibrato can be controlled. I have taught thousands of singers how to develop and control vibrato, whether they had no vibrato, an uneven, erratic vibrato, or an uncontrolled vocal fold flutter vibrato. Vibrato must be controlled if your goal is to have a professional career in singing. Can you imagine a cellist or a flautist leaving vibrato to "chance?" Or expecting vibrato to come naturally?

I have used the term "Diaphragmatic vibrato" since 1976 and I continue to use the term "Diaphragmatic vibrato," because I feel that although the diaphragmatic muscle is involuntary and not actually producing the vibrato, the breath mechanism is responsible for the control of this vibrato and that the diaphragm is involved.

Diaphragmatic Vibrato - "On the Breath"

Recently, I spoke to a professional flautist and bassoonist and the term they use for the even, wave-like sound of vibrato on the breath is "diaphragmatic vibrato." They also called it "abdominal vibrato." The problem with using the term, "abdominal," is that I would not want to have singers believe that the whole lower stomach pulsates with each pulse of vibrato. That would surely produce a vibrato too slow and too wide. So I am very careful to point out that pulses are felt in the solar plexus area, a small area about 3 inches in diameter right beneath the breast bone.

These musicians have also mentioned that there are other types of vibrato for flute and clarinet that are done with the lips, jaw, and/or throat. Once you learn to sing with diaphragmatic vibrato, try it out on a flute. I did, and I felt immediately at home. You will feel like you are singing through an instrument!

The term diaphragmatic vibrato on the breath describes the feeling the singer has when sustaining a long note with a free-flowing vibrato that feels like it is floating on air, with very little throat muscle involvement. It is created by slight, almost *imperceptible*, solar plexus outward pulsations in a small area about 3 inches in diameter right beneath the breast bone, while maintaining firm support and by resisting collapse of the ribs as they slowly return to their natural state. Diaphragmatic vibrato on the breath is heard in every vocal style from blues, R&B, jazz, rock, music theater and classical.

These pulses cause the air to flow through the vocal folds in a wave-like motion, creating slight fluctuations in pitch and volume. On the pulse, the volume is louder. Between pulses, the volume is softer. On the pulse the pitch is dead center. Between pulses the pitch is slightly lower. The fluctuations in pitch should be so minute that we can't really hear the changes. This fluctuation in pitch and volume gives a sensual quality to the sustained tone.

Diaphragmatic vibrato on the breath allows you to control the speed of your vibrato. You can sing with a faster, slower, slow to fast, wider or more narrow vibrato. Crescendos and decrescendos will become easier and more fun to sing.

With diaphragmatic vibrato on the breath, you'll find it possible to sustain your high notes with a feeling that is nearly effortless and sounds effortless. Because you are using your breathing and support muscles to create vibrato, with much less throat and tongue involvement, you will experience a sense of freedom of tone and more ability to express your music. Diaphragmatic vibrato on the breath helps to free the tone. It helps to stay on pitch. Sustaining a note effortlessly with an even vibrato shouldn't be a hope and a prayer. It is a skill and we singers must recognize vibrato as a tool of expression. The type of vibrato and whether to use it or not is your choice as an artist. It depends on your personal taste and musical style.

For many years, I have used the image of a big beach ball pulsating evenly on top of a water fountain to create the image of "vibrato on the breath." A few years ago at the International Congress of Voice Teachers (ICVT) in Helsinki, Finland, I heard the great Wagnerian soprano, Birgit Nilsson describe vibrato as "a little ball bouncing on top of a water spout." I was thrilled!

Some well known singers can be recognized by the uniqueness of their vibrato. It can even be their trademark. But surprisingly few singers are aware of how they produce their vibrato. No one is born with a natural vibrato. It is learned.

Vibrato: An Element of Style

Once you become aware of all the variations in vibrato techniques, you will be able to recognize the different types of vibrato used in all areas of vocal music. For example, R&B (rhythm & blues) singers, in general, use a slower vibrato on sustained tones than opera singers. Jazz singers use several vibrato techniques. Rock singers use less vibrato than classical singers. It also depends on the song. This is why you can't go from an operatic aria to a rock song and sing it with the same technique. Classical training is a good foundation, but one must then study musical style in order to sing a specific, non-classical style authentically. Vibrato is an important element of vocal style.

Vibrato Speed

Vibrato speed may vary from song to song and also within the same song, changing with the emotional expression. Usually, a slower vibrato is used in a slower song and a faster vibrato in a faster song. A slower vibrato is calming. A faster vibrato is exciting. Speeding up the vibrato as you sustain a tone increases the energy and intensity of the sound and emotion. The ability to control the speed of your vibrato gives you more options in creating your own style.

The Straight Tone

The straight tone is a sustained tone without vibrato. In commercial/pop music the straight tone is an integral part of vocal expression and emotional coloration. Melodic lines of quarter notes or shorter duration are usually straight tones. A sustained tone often begins with a straight tone that moves gradually into a vibrato. This is called delayed vibrato
(———⋀⋀⋀).
A word like "blue" in "I'm so blue," would probably be sung with a delayed vibrato to describe a sad feeling. A shimmering vibrato would indicate high energy and would not describe a sad feeling. A high energy shimmering vibrato would be appropriate in a word like "Sunny."

Note: The clearer the vowel, the easier the vibrato. The vocal folds will focus on a clearly pronounced open vowel sound better than on an unclear vowel sound. When the balance between the air pressure and focused vocal folds is correct, it is much easier to control vibrato. I remember when I had a voice studio in Manhattan, I had the pleasure of having a visit from Jack De Lon, a well known Broadway tenor who was at that time appearing at City Center as "Mr. Snow," in a revival of "Carousel." He was touted as one of the best "Mr. Snow's" ever, and as he left my studio he said, "Remember, sing on the vowel!" He was so right.

Exercises for Diaphragmatic Vibrato: "Vibrato on the Breath"

(Singing Techniques CD, Track 17)

1. Using the exclamation, "Hey!" send out an easy, "shout-like" sound, as if calling to someone across a crowded room. Strive for a balance in the out and down sensation of the support muscles with good focus and forward placement. Listen for the ring and feel the buzz. Don't force!

2. Without stopping the tone, send out a "Hey!" with 2 pulses.

   He-ey! (not Hey!-hey!)

   You should feel subtle pulses as a slight but definite outward action (not pulling up and in) in the area of the solar plexus. Keep your rib cage up and open. Don't let it collapse, or move up and down with the pulses. The abdominal muscles should maintain a gentle firmness, not rigid and not bouncing. Don't close the throat or vocal folds to end a sustained tone. End the sound using the last vibrato pulse. Make it sound as though it vanished into "thin air" and not clipped, coughed or choked off. Keep the pulses even. Feel the jaw relaxed and flexible. You can also use a hiss (s s s s) or (f f f f) or "shhh" sound instead of the "Hey!" to practice the vibrato. Alternating between pulsing the hiss and pulsing the vocal sound is an effective way of developing vibrato control.

3. Now increase the number of pulses (If you have a metronome, you can use it to help keep the pulses even):

3 pulses:

s - s - s   He- e- ey!

5 pulses:

s- s- s- s- s   He- e- e- e- ey!

9 pulses:

s- s- s- s- s- s- s- s- s   He- e- e- e- e- e- e- ey!

As note values, this exercise would read as follows:

At first, choose a medium pitch at a medium volume, so that you will more easily be able to feel the support. As you progress, try other variations... high notes, low notes, loud, soft.
Check with your finger tips to make sure you're not bouncing the support muscles. Keep your rib cage up and open. Don't let the pitch vary or wobble. Think of the vibrato as always smooth and moving forward.

4. In head voice, using the vowel "ee",
Sing:

5. Using the hisses as a preparation, three times in a row,
Sing:

In head voice, three times in a row,
Sing:

(Singing Techniques CD, Track 18)

6. Using the words "on and on," in lower register,
   Sing:

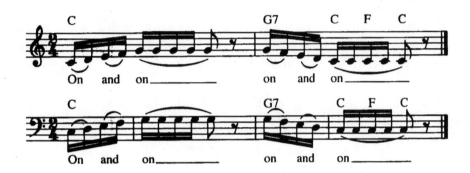

7. In head voice, using the words "you and me,"
   Sing:

Repeat this exercise, moving up a half step at a time. Vary word combinations and vary volume. Use the practice phrases on page 133.

8. Now let's use *delayed vibrato*, that is, a straight tone followed by pulses on each sustained note. Use a single vowel "ah" or "eh," first loud, then soft, and feel the pulses as 4 sixteenth notes on the last beat of each measure.
   Sing:

9. Repeat, moving up in half steps using your practice phrases.

10. Sing the following exercises in various parts of your range, using the practice phrases.
    Sing:

11. Using a slow song, choose the words that you would like to sustain and practice them using 3, 5, 9 or more pulses of vibrato depending on how long you hold the note.

12. Also in your song, practice delayed vibrato. For example,
    Sing:

Work on speeding up and slowing down the vibrato rate, keeping a smooth, gradual flow with even pulses. In performance, you would not count pulses, but as a practice technique, this is an excellent way of perfecting your vibrato control. A singer with diaphragmatic vibrato control can use the vibrato speed to match the desired emotional energy level of the song. Mastering the diaphragmatic vibrato may take time and patience, but the results are very rewarding.

Note: Diaphragmatic vibrato alone cannot produce an extremely rapid vibrato. Throat and/or shimmering vibrato must be added.

Sustaining Diphthongs With Vibrato

(Singing Techniques CD, Tracks 19)

When sustaining a tone on a diphthong, which is two vowel sounds back to back, we sustain the first vowel sound and sing the second vowel sound at the end. For example, in the word, "my," the dipthong is [ai]. We would sing it like this "maaaaaai," rather than "maiiiiiiii." You can soften the [i] sound by using [ɪ] (as in *him*). For example, [maⁱ]. Make sure the tip of your tongue rests behind your lower teeth and the middle of your tongue rises against your upper molars toward the middle of your mouth. Your jaw should not move the tongue up and down. The tongue needs to be independent from your jaw. In the word, "so," the diphthong is [ɔᵁ]. We would sing it like this, "sɔᵁ" rather than "sɔu." You can soften the [u] sound in the dipthongs ending with [u], by using [ʊ] as in (*book*).

Exercise

1. Choose a single pitch. Using the words on this list, sustain the first vowel sound and tag on the second sound with the consonant after the final vibrato pulse.

(Singing Techniques CD, Track 20)

Sing:

<u>International Phonetic Alphabet (I.P.A.)</u>
I.P.A. symbols below in parentheses

(smiled) sm<u>ahee</u>ld	[ai]	or	[aˡ]
(boy) b<u>awee</u>	[ɔi]	or	[ɔˡ]
(moist) m<u>awee</u>st	[ɔi]	or	[ɔˡ]
(day) d<u>ehee</u>	[ɛi]	or	[ɛˡ]
(face) f<u>ehee</u>ce	[ɛi]	or	[ɛˡ]
(now) na<u>aaa</u>oo	[æ]	or	[æ^ʊ]
(cloud) cla<u>aaa</u>ood	[æ]	or	[æ^ʊ]
(so) s<u>awoo</u>	[ɔu]	or	[ɔ^ʊ]
(home) h<u>awoo</u>m	[ɔu]	or	[ɔ^ʊ]

Consonant "R"

Watch out for the consonant "r" following a vowel or a diphthong. The tendency is to close the vowel and go to the "r" too soon, as in the word, "hard." For example, "Harrrrrrd." Stay on the open vowel [a] and save the "rd" for after the final pulse of vibrato. However, in country western style, singing on the "r" might be more authentic.

Sing:

Haaaaaaaaard

Sustaining Consonants with Vibrato

In commercial/pop music, sustaining a consonant with vibrato can be expressive. For example, holding the "M" and "n" in "<u>My</u> m<u>an</u>," or the "l" and "n," in "Alone," can be very effective. The way in which words are sustained and the choice of vibrato technique should be considered in developing your personal style.

Throat Vibrato Exercise

The simplest way to feel the sensation of the throat vibrato is to first start off with the interval of the minor 3rd, for example C to A. Sing a sustained tone and move quickly back and forth from C to A. For example,
Sing:

C - A - C - A - C - A - C

Now decrease the interval to a major 2nd. For example,
Sing:

SING!

C - B♭ - C - B♭ - C - B♭ - C - B♭

Now, decrease the interval to the minor 2nd. For example,

Sing:

C - B - C - B - C - B - C

Finally, try a very minute change in pitch ... about a 1/4 interval or less. The fluctuation in pitch should not be noticeable.

Helpful Hints for Diaphragmatic Vibrato on the Breath

1. If you find that you cannot speed up the diaphragmatic vibrato it means that the focusing strength of the vocal folds and the breath pressure is not in balance.
2. The last pulse of vibrato, whether on a vowel, consonant, forte, piano, crescendo or decrescendo should be an energetic "send off."
3. Keep your body quiet. Don't pulse your head, jaw, ribs or abdomen with the vibrato.
4. The better the balance of air pressure and vocal fold adduction, the better the result. A clear vowel will help focus the vocal folds.
5. The tone should be smooth and the pulsations of the vibrato not *obvious*. It takes subtle pulses to produce the desired effect. The result is a vibrato that feels natural, free, smooth and "on the breath."
6. Make sure that as you sing, the rib cage resists collapse and returns to its original position gradually. If the support is lax, the vibrato will slow down and will become a wobble.
7. You can practice your vibrato on the breath without sound by using a *hiss*, keeping the pulsations smooth.
8. You can practice your shimmering vibrato by using short, staccato notes.
9. Vibrato on the breath depends on a clear, focused vowel.

   Note: As you increase the speed of the diaphragmatic vibrato, you will see that some throat vibrato will be engaged. This can not be avoided. Diaphragmatic vibrato alone can not produce a very fast vibrato, but it should be combined with some throat vibrato for the fast sustained tones. For the fastest moving notes, shimmering vibrato is appropriate.

Tongue Release Exercise

If you are having trouble keeping your vibrato *even*, or if the pitch *flats*, it is usually because the root of your tongue is engaged and is trying to control the vibrato. If there is undue tongue pressure, the pitch will flat because the tongue tension affects the vocal folds, thus altering the pitch.

Here is a tongue release exercise which will release tongue tension. When we stretch out the back of the tongue, tension is released and this allows the pulsations of breath to happen freely. You can use the tongue release exercise for working on sustaining tones with diaphragmatic vibrato. It can also be used for scales and arpeggios. My students call it a "miracle" exercise because they experience immediate results.

Three steps:

1. Use a damp, paper towel and hold the front part of your tongue stretched out while doing each vibrato exercise.
2. Next, hold the tongue out *without* the paper towel while doing the same vibrato exercise.

3. Sing the vowel "ah" with the tongue in a normal relaxed position while doing the same vibrato exercise.
   Use this exercise on vowels in words of songs.

Background On Vibrato

* "Closely related to vibrato is the soft variety of the so-called Caccini *trillo* or *trilletto* in which there is no *coup de glotte* ('stroke of the glottis') - the *trillo* itself has a coup de glotte and is thus not a vibrato, but a staccato repetition. A different version of the trill or mordent is the *chevrotement* ('goat's trill'), against which many treatises on singing issue stern warnings ('il caprino fa ridere')." "Il caprino fa ridere" is Italian literally translated, "the goat makes to laugh." The *chevrotement,* is from the French verb, *"chevroter:* to bleat; to sing or speak in a quavering voice."** *Chevrotement* is similar to the more rapid vocal fold flutter vibrato.

The Flamenco singers of Spain, as well as many of the Middle Eastern singers, use vocal fold flutter vibrato, but not exclusively, and is also typical of the French chanteuse or cabaret singer, such as in the singing of the legendary Edith Piaf. There are also recordings of her singing with a "diaphragmatic on the breath vibrato" as well as "throat vibrato."

The straight tone can be heard in Early Church music, such as in the Gregorian Chant (9th-13th centuries) and in Church Music in the 14th and 15th centuries. One reason for using a straight tone in church music might be because of the echo effect in a church. With a straight tone there is no fluctuation of pitch, as in a tone with vibrato, therefore the melody can be heard clearly.

Straight tone is typically used when singing the music of the Renaissance period (1450-1600) by composers such as Palestrina and Josquin des Prez. These works are still performed in that manner today.

As we approached the 19th century, the music of the Romantic period began to reflect more sensuality in all vocal styles, including art songs (poems set to music) and opera. Vibrato was considered an expression of the word and therefore it became an essential element of the Romantic style. It is inconceivable that an aria from "La Traviata," "La Boheme" or "Cavalleria Rusticana" would be performed without vibrato.

The type of vibrato even varied from one culture to another. A slightly wider and slower vibrato was more typical of the Italian style of singing, compared to the faster and less wide vibrato of the French or German style.

In the operas of Richard Wagner and Richard Strauss, opera singers often use a straight tone, moving into a diaphragmatic or shimmering vibrato. The effect is a powerfully piercing and intense quality, well suited to the heroic roles of the late 19th century and early 20th century German Opera. Wagner wrote for the voice as if it were an instrument, part of the total musical fabric of the orchestra. Because of the tremendous size of the orchestra used in most of his works, a sizeable voice with well focused vocal folds having an *edge,* a voice like "steel," combined with the use of diaphragmatic and shimmer vibrato, became necessary for projection in these heroic operas.

In the 20th Century vocal music of composers such as Arnold Schoenberg ("Pierrot Lunaire"), Alban Berg ("Lulu") and Kurt Weill ("Three Penny Opera"), the straight tone without vibrato represents speech-like sounds and is just as expressive as singing with vibrato. A good

SING!

example of this style of singing is voice of Lotte Lenya, who made her mark starring in works such as "The Three Penny Opera" by Kurt Weill.

In operetta, a precursor of the Broadway Musical, particularly in the female voices (Jeannette McDonald and Kathryn Grayson), the vocal fold flutter was typical. As we approached the mid 20th century, Broadway performers such as Ethel Merman, Richard Kiley, Barbara Cook and John Raitt brought the more operatic style of *diaphragmatic* and *shimmer vibrato* to the Broadway style of singing. They also used straight tone, to represent speech-like sounds.

For comic character roles, vibrato can be used to fit the character: Vocal fold flutter, shimmering vibrato, throat vibrato, very wide vibrato, no vibrato, etc.

Since vibrato is so much a part of musical style and personal expression, it is truly an interesting study. I recommend learning all four vibrato techniques taught in this book: Diaphragmatic vibrato on the breath, throat vibrato, vocal fold flutter vibrato and shimmering vibrato.

I have been singing with and teaching diaphragmatic vibrato throughout my singing and teaching career and I am happy to say that diaphragmatic vibrato has been a major factor in freeing throat and tongue tension in many of my students who have gone on to professional singing careers, and may not have had the same opportunities using an uncontrolled vibrato.

Happy singing!

* The New Grove Dictionary of Opera, edited by Stanley Sadie, volume 4.
** The Bantam New College French and English Dictionary

CHAPTER SEVEN

Good Vibrations!
Vocal Colors
Resonance

"Liz Howard and the Vocal Power Method have drastically improved my voice. Working with Liz really helped strengthen my voice and broaden my style. She is truly the best in the biz!"

Hadas
Semi-Finalist, 2003 American Idol
Winner, 2003 Pantene Pro-Voice Award

(Singing Techniques CD, Tracks 21-27)

The Vocal Tract

The voice, like all acoustic instruments, such as the guitar, trumpet, piano, or violin, has its own special chambers for resonating the tone. "Sound waves can resonate only in an open/closed tube like the vocal tract."* As you may recall from an earlier chapter, the vocal tract extends from the vocal folds to the lip opening.

"To this point, the vocal tract has been idealized a tube of uniform diameter that is closed at one end and open at the other. As the sound moves through the vocal tract, it encounters several places where the size of the resonating chamber changes. Many of these changes in shape are under the direct control of the singer. Movements of the tongue, jaw, soft palate, and pharyngeal wall all translate into resonance changes. The pharynx is the resonator above the larynx and behind the mouth, consisting of laryngo-, oro- and naso-pharynges."*

Once the tone is produced by the breath, (power source), it passes through the vibrating vocal folds (vibrator), then it resonates in the vocal tract (resonator).

Even though we feel vibrations in the chest and head, these areas are not open/closed tubes. The vibrations may seem like resonance, but they are vibrations that resonate in the vocal tract. However, for our purposes, I will refer to these areas as...

The Four Primary Colors:

1) chest   2) mouth   3) nasal/mask   4) head

The "Placement Track" Exercise

Think of the colors as being on a "placement track." In the lower range, the chest vibrations are felt more easily, which naturally produce a darker color. In the middle range, the mouth vibrations are felt more easily and produce a speech-like color. As we proceed a little higher in our range, our nasal vibrations are felt more easily and produce a mask/nasal color. In the higher range, the vibrations in the head produce a lighter color.

These colors can be used any where in the range in any register and at any volume level to produce emotional effects in the performance of a song or aria. Exception: pure head color can only be soft.

Here is an exercise you can do to feel the colors in your placement track:

Begin on a low note and using the open vowel "ah," slide your voice slowly up, beginning with your chest color, through your mouth color, then nasal color and finally head color. You can let your voice move into your head register (falsetto) as you approach your head color.

* Excerpt from "Your Voice: An Inside View," by Scott McCoy, DM.

By isolating these colors through exercises, you will have a better understanding of how you can use these colors to express emotions in your music. The word or emotional content of the phrase encourage the choice of colors and it is you, the artist, who makes the choices.

Chest Color

Chest color is felt as vibrations in the chest and resonates in the vocal tract. It used for a darker, deeper tone. Added to the other three colors, along with more vocal fold adduction and breath pressure, chest color accomplishes maximum volume.

Mouth Color

Mouth color is a resonance and is used for conversational tones, typically in the mid-range.

Nasal Color

Nasal color is a resonance that is present in a well produced tone, except, perhaps, in the instance of the pure head color. Nasal resonance is bright and "edgy," and is important in achieving *mask* resonance. Nasal resonance helps the vocal folds to focus (adduct), and therefore helps to give clarity to the tone. Pure nasal resonance is rarely used, except for comic character voices in music theater or opera.

Head Color

Head color is felt as vibrations in the head and resonates in the vocal tract. Head color should not be confused with head register or falsetto (page 65). Head color is used primarily for softer singing.

There are singers who are recognized by their pronounced nasal quality and others noted for a deep, dark and chesty sound and still others for their breathy or heady sound... and so on.

The quality or color of your voice also depends on your skill in the use of these various resonances and colors by controlling the shape of your *vocal tract*.

It has been demonstrated, electrographically in the form of "voice prints," that like fingerprints, no two voices are exactly alike.

Exercises for Placement

Note: For the following exercises, "low voice" will refer to the lower male range and "high voice" will refer to the higher male range and the female mid-range. Exercises not labeled are for all voices. On the CDs you will hear "chest and head resonance." In this book they are referred to as "colors." It is the vibrations in these areas that will give us the desired color.

Head Color

Yawn and feel the open sensation in your throat as the soft palate lifts and the space widens between the back of your tongue and the roof of your mouth. Don't pull your tongue back or lift the back of your tongue. The tip of the tongue should rest behind the lower teeth except to move away momentarily to articulate consonants like "t," "d," "l," "n," "sh," etc. The yawning sensation also allows the focusing strength of the vocal folds to relax for softer tones.

(Singing Techniques CD, Track 21)

1. Feel as though you are aiming the tone straight up behind an arched soft palate. Keep your tongue relaxed and forward and with the yawn sensation. Listen for a sound that is light, heady and clearly focused (not breathy). Use a firm, steady, out and down support but very little air pressure. Feel the vocal folds vibrate and call out gently:

a) "Hey!" (like a far-away shout)

b) " ooooo " (like an owl in the distance)

c) " eeeee " (with the same quality)

In the following exercises repeated notes represent vibrato pulses.

(Singing Techniques CD, Track 22)

2. In lower chest voice using head color, very softly,
Sing:

3. In the upper chest voice for men and medium range chest voice for women,
using head color, very softly,
Sing:

4. Use your head voice or soprano (falsetto for men), very softly,
Sing:

Additional Exercises

1. On a comfortable pitch in head voice and using the delayed vibrato, very softly,
Sing: "oo" (as in m<u>oo</u>n):

Sing: "ee" (as in s<u>ee</u>):

After you establish these head colors, try other vowel sounds, then words. When a word starts with a vowel, begin the tone with a "silent H" to avoid a glottal attack at the onset of the tone.

2. Match the heady quality of the "oo" and "ee" in the vowel of the word that follows.

   "ah" vowel sound (as in *far*)

   oo ... oo ... fa - a - a - a - a - a - a - a - ar

   ee ... ee ... fa- a -a -a -a -a -a -a - ar

3. Now use the word "*Hello.*"

   oo ... oo ... hello - o - o - o - o - o - o - o

   ee ... ee ... hello - o - o - o - o - o - o - o

4. In head color,
   Sing:

5. Continue, using the practice phrases on page 133.

Nasal and Mask Resonance

Placing a tone "forward," or "in the mask," is a commonly used description of how it feels to resonate in the bony structures around the nose, eyes and cheekbones. Nasal resonance is vitally important in achieving mask resonance. We must first isolate the nasal resonance. As was mentioned previously, the pure nasal tone is mostly used for comic character voices or special effects. Even when emphasizing another color, such as chest color, if your intention is to project your voice at a louder volume, the mask resonance must still be present.

It is interesting to note here that a singer with a cold usually refers to herself or himself as being "nasal" when in fact the sound is "de-nasalized." The resonating spaces are "stopped-up" and actually are *not* vibrating freely.

The "Inner Smile"

To assist in accomplishing the forward placement (mask resonance), imagine an "inner smile" in the cheek bone area. Don't grimace or distort your facial expression. This "inner smile" helps to keep the tone forward and clear. Remember to always sing on the clear, open vowel sound for a better understanding of the word by your audience and for the vocal folds to vibrate more efficiently.

Good Vibrations! Vocal Colors: Resonance   59

Exercises

Let the back of the soft palate relax or drop. Let the back of the tongue rise slightly. Think the sound "ng" as in the word, "sing." The "aa" vowel sound (as in <u>a</u>t [æ]) is very helpful in activating the nasal resonance and achieving singing in the mask. The consonants "n," "m" and "ng" assist the process since they require nasal opening.

1. Think the sound "ng" (as in <u>ang</u>le) and say strongly,

"aaaaa, aaaaa, aaaaa"

2. Now an octave higher, in head voice,
Sing:

Notice that thinking "ng" brings the tongue closer to the soft palate. This allows the nasal resonance to be felt more easily since the tone is partly channeled through the nasal passage.

1. On a comfortable pitch using pure nasal resonance, with 9 pulses of vibrato,
Sing a - a - (as in <u>ha</u>t) [æ].

$$na \text{-} a \text{-} a \text{-} a \text{-} a \text{-} a \text{-} a \text{-} a \text{-} a$$
$$(\quad \sim\!\sim\!\sim\!\sim\!\sim\!\sim\!\sim \quad)$$

2. Using "aa" to establish the mask resonance, sing various words containing the "aa" vowel. Use 9 pulses of vibrato.
Sing:

la - a - a - a - a - a - a - and

gra-a-a- a-a- a-a- a- ass

3. Using "aa … aa…" as a set-up for the placement, change the vowel to "eh" (as in <u>end</u>) [ɛ] and keep the placement the same.
Sing:

Continue with other vowel sounds using the list on page 30.

4. Sing:

(Singing Techniques CD, Track 24)

5. Use your head color followed by head and nasal resonance combined (lower chest voice).
   Sing:

6. An octave higher (high chest voice).
   Sing:

7. And in the head voice (high and low voices).
   Sing:

9. Continue with the list of practice phrases on page 133, maintaining mask resonance.

Mouth Resonance

(Singing Techniques CD, Track 25)

1. With a natural, hearty speech-like quality, say "*Hi!*" through a smiling mouth. Feel the open vowel sound vibrating against the upper front teeth. Use the "inner smile," with a conversational approach.

2. Say: "*Hey!*" (against the teeth).

3. In mouth resonance,
   Sing: (low chest voice)

4. An octave higher.

Sing: (high chest voice)

5. And in head voice.

Sing: (low and high voices)

6. Move on to other vowel sounds using the practice phrases on page 133. Speak these sounds at first with a natural, hearty quality and then go on to sustain a tone on a single pitch. When emphasizing the mouth resonance, you should feel the presence of the other resonances, particularly nasal and chest.

Chest Color

The chest color should not be confused with chest register or chest voice. It is the darkest of the vocal colors and can be used throughout the entire vocal range.

Chest color is used for emotions such as power, confidence, strength, and sensuality. To increase chest resonance, open your throat wide as in a yawn. This will widen the throat resonating space, lowering the larynx and lifting the soft palate. When the larynx is lowered, the vocal tract becomes longer, hence the darker color. It's like comparing a soprano saxophone to a baritone saxophone. The longer the resonating space, the deeper the color.

Do not press the tongue down or pull it back in your throat as sometimes happens in a real yawn. It helps to think the sound, "uh," as in the word, "under." Feel your chest bones vibrating by putting the palm of your hand on your chest bones as you do these exercises. There is a tendency for the vocal folds to relax their focusing strength when we sing with more chest color. Be careful not to lose the adduction in your vocal folds as you widen the throat space.

Make sure that you are utilizing the mouth and nasal resonance simultaneously with the chest color to maintain the brilliance and projection of the tone. A pure chest color without nasality could be rather unattractive, unless you are using that sound for a special effect.

Note to the ladies: Don't be afraid to use chest color in your singing. Don't worry about sounding "like a man." Chest color in any voice type adds a beautiful and deep richness to the voice in any part of the range and in any register, chest, head or mix!

(Singing Techniques CD, Track 26)

1. Using a dark, angry, shout-like tone, think the sound "uh" (as in _under_) [ʌ]. Feel your chest bones vibrating, and call out:

   Hey!

2. Now repeat in your head voice.

   Hey!

(Singing Techniques CD, Track 27)

3. Now add the chest color to the head, nasal and mouth colors.
Sing: (low chest voice)

4. Using chest color, an octave higher,
Sing: (high chest voice)

5. Now with a shift to the brighter resonances at the top of the scale, emphasizing the nasal and head colors.
Sing: (high chest voice)

6. Using head voice (falsetto), emphasize the chest color.
Sing:

7. Here's an exercise that begins with the head color, then adds nasal, then mouth, then chest. Low chest voices first:
Sing:

8. And an octave higher.
Sing:

9. And in upper register (head voice).
Sing:

Helpful Hints

1. Never "push" your air pressure beyond the point of clarity of tone. The "ring" from vibrating focused vocal folds and mask resonance is necessary for the projection of the tone.
2. When bringing the chest color up to the higher notes be careful to stay "on top" of the pitch as there is a tendency to sing under the pitch using too much chest color. *Anchor* the tone in the mask resonance when adding chest color.
3. If you are practicing mouth resonance and your intention is to crescendo, try to add volume without changing your mouth resonance. The color remains the same, only the volume changes. This is for practicing one color at a time.
4. Head color alone is soft and you can only crescendo by adding other colors along with added air pressure and added vocal fold adduction (at the same time).
5. You can sing with any resonance in any register. You have four distinct resonances/colors that can be used in your chest, head, or mix registers.

Three Other "Colors"

The vocal tract, as mentioned before in the chapter on breathing and support, is the area from the glottis (vocal folds) to the lips. The vocal tract can take on different shapes according to the placement of the tongue, the raising or lowering of the soft palate, the lowering of the larynx, the widening of the throat, and the opening and closing of the jaw. Singers have the ability to create various vocal colors by the altering the shape of our vocal tracts.

The "Back L"

The *Back L* (my term) is a vocal quality that is heard in commercial/pop singing including country western, blues, R&B and jazz. The *Back L* has nothing to do with singing "l" in a word. How do we sing a *Back L*? Here's how: If you exaggerate the pronunciation of the "l" in the word, "wall," you will discover the *Back L*. A good example of the *Back L,* can be heard in the singing of Leann Rimes, who uses the *Back L* very effectively in much of her singing. You can use the *Back L* also to sing higher notes in chest voice with a rounder, richer sound. However, too much *Back L* can be disturbing to the ear. The *Back L* should not be used throughout an entire piece, since it gives a one dimensional impression of the singer's vocal quality.

The "Throat Cry" and "Throat Laugh"

The feeling of a "cry" or a "laugh" in your vocal tract will add a tremendous emotional quality to your singing. You can create a quality in your voice that gives chills to listeners. This sound can be described as "a tear (from the eye) in the voice."

I believe that a singer must fall in love with his or her own voice and that even when we sing our scales and exercises, that "cry" or "laugh" must be there. Otherwise, the sound is mechanically produced without real beauty of tone and expression.

The "Creaky Door"

The *Creaky door* (my term) is a sound commonly found in styles from classical to blues and is used to express pain, suffering, longing, etc. The vocal folds are brought together just enough with slight sub-glottic air pressure as to mimic the sound of a creaky door.

Every Note Deserves to Live!

When you watch a great cellist, you can see that he is feeling every note of the music, as his body moves with the music. His right bow arm is expressive and seems to speak to us through skillful movements across the strings. As his left hand moves up and down the neck of the cello for the various notes, we can see that vibrato is so clearly a musical expression. In his autobiography, the legendary cellist Pablo Casals is quoted as saying, "Although it is pp, every note must sing!" "Not one note dry." "A sense of wonder." "Let the wave follow its natural urge towards the crest." "Generally, a long note means crescendo or diminuendo. The note has to say something firm, expression, interest."

CHAPTER EIGHT

Lower and Upper Registers

"Elisabeth Howard's "VOCAL POWER" technique has opened new avenues to my teaching of singing... better results have been achieved much faster than with any other technique which I have used during my twenty-eight years of teaching voice."

Vera do Canto e Mello
Brazilian Association of Teachers of Singing
Performer; Fulbright Scholar, Vocal Pedagogy, University of Indiana

Our Registers

Both male and female voices have two distinct registers or "qualities" of sound: the lower register and the upper register. The lower register is also referred to as any of the following: chest voice, lower voice, speaking voice, modal, alto voice and belt voice. The upper register is referred to as any of the following: The head voice, upper voice, legit voice, soprano and falsetto, which is a term more commonly associated with the highest tones in the male voice, resembling the female soprano quality. The head voice refers to register and should not be confused with head resonance, which refers to color. The chest voice refers to register and should not be confused with chest *color*.

The "Break"

Many singers experience a *break*, or sudden change in the vocal sound when proceeding from one register to the other. This change or *"break"* takes place in the area where the registers overlap. This area of transition is also called the *passaggio,* which in Italian means "passing, crossing, transition in music, transfer." In singing, the passaggio is the transition between registers. There is no <u>one</u> note where one register begins and the other ends.

Within this overlap area, we have the higher notes of the chest voice and the lower notes of the head voice. However, in this passaggio area, a blending or mixing of the registers is possible. With the exercises in this book and practice, you can learn how to blend from one register to the other with no apparent or abrupt change in quality.

Blending chest and head registers

The vocal folds for the louder chest register tones require more focusing strength (firmness) than the same notes in the head register. Therefore, if you are singing loudly from chest to head in the same range, you will not be able to match the quality from chest to head, but rather you will experience an abrupt change in quality or a "break." The vocal folds will suddenly release from chest register to head register.

If you are singing in head register on a downward musical line into the lower register, and if you carry the head register too low, you will not be heard unless you are able to match the tone quality of the head register with the chest register.

A transition between upper and lower registers without an apparent break can be achieved by controlling the balance of air pressure and vocal fold focusing strength.

When making a transition in either direction, ascending from chest to head register, or descending from head to chest register, widen the throat space by lifting the soft palate and thinking "uh," as in "under." At the same time, add air pressure for a smooth transition.

Widening the throat space helps to make a smoother vocal fold transition from one register to the other.

Helpful Hints:

1. Ascending, gradually decrease the focusing strength of the vocal folds in the chest register as you move into the head register while widening the throat space. Add air pressure at the same time.
2. Descending, gradually increase the focusing strength of the vocal folds as you move into the chest register while widening the throat space. Add air pressure at the same time.
3. Keep your support steady and sing a clear vowel.
4. Don't let your tongue press down in the back of your throat as you think "uh" [ʌ] as in "under."

Try it out on an ascending scale and then a descending scale. In either direction, this works well. Make sure you don't bring the chest register too high and loud. Then try it in a song!

CHAPTER NINE

The Pop Sound Belt Mix

"Liz Howard's teaching technique has given my voice more range, clarity and flexibility than ever before. My voice has improved the most and in the shortest amount of time under Liz' direction."

Drew Bell
T.V.'s "The Bold & the Beautiful," "Jeepers Creepers 2"

Photo by Michael Calas

(Singing Techniques CD, Track 28-29)

The *belt mix* is used to camouflage the break area, to blend registers and to sing high, powerful notes that match the chest register. The belt mix is the same for both female and male singers in commercial/pop vocal styles from blues, R&B and rock, to country, jazz and gospel. The belt mix is also used in music theatre songs that require high, full volume singing that matches the chest register above the chest register range. The belt mix is also used by tenors and baritones in classical singing and is referred to in Italian as *la voce mista*, and in French, *la voix mixte*.

We already learned how to blend from chest register into head register. Here's how it works from chest register into mix:

As we ascend the scale, beginning on a lower note in chest register, we begin with firm vocal folds and *gradually decrease* the firmness as we move into the upper range. In order for the belt mix to sound like chest register, the *belt mix* must be anchored in the mask. The mask resonance helps to match the sound of the chest register. I refer to the belt mix as our "safety zone." (I also call this "the Elisabeth Howard throat by-pass"!) The belt mix requires firm and steady support. The lower back muscles stay firm. This is *safe belting*, not harmful to the voice. *Unsafe belting* is when the vocal folds are held firm too high in the range, and are *not gradually released* for the higher notes, resulting in a forced or strained sound. This creates undue strain on the vocal folds. Holding the firmness in the vocal folds too high is what causes the "break" to occur because the vocal folds are obliged to suddenly release when it gets too high for the chest register and you find yourself "breaking" into looser vocal folds, creating a pure head register, not matched to the chest register. Bringing full chest register too high without the mix is also what causes the "cracking" into falsetto in male voices. For blending the chest register into mix, belt mix is used just below the break area and continues throughout the passaggio into the higher range.

Now, if you want to "yodel" in traditional country music style, you can use this abrupt change from head to chest register. Abrupt changes in registers can be also be used effectively, especially in blues, rock, R&B and alternative styles, so it isn't necessarily something to avoid, but can be used as an element of expression. In 20th Century classical singing, "voice cracking" between registers is used for emotional effect. The break is used for comic effect in the Rossini "Figaro" aria.

The register break for the female Pop singer or Broadway belter, takes place in the area between A above middle C and the D above that, but varies with the individual. The female belt mix can go as high as two F's above middle C–and even higher in some individuals. Having a good belt mix on the F, two F's above middle C, is as high as you need to sing. The female belt mix can be heard on an F, two F's above middle C, at the very end of "The Life of the Party," sung by Idina Menzel from the Broadway show, on the original cast recording of *The Wild Party.*

For men, the register break generally occurs somewhere between F above middle C and the B flat above that, but varies with the individual. There is a good example of a high G in belt mix, two G's above middle C in Gesthemanes' Song from the Broadway show, *Jesus Christ Super Star,* sung by Ian Gillian in the London recording. Very few singers can sing this high in belt mix, so don't think you must sing a high G to be a good singer.

R&B male and female singers use belt mix in most of their singing. In R&B, you could hear chest register, head register and belt mix all in the same song. The belt mix is typical in gospel singing. Aretha Franklin, who began as a gospel singer and made a professional career in pop/R&B, uses belt mix very effectively throughout her singing in both gospel and pop/R&B. Listen to her recording of "Respect."

Take your time with the exercises for belt mix. Don't rush or push your voice too high, too soon. It usually takes several months. Practice your belt mix in your practice sessions five times a week and only 5-10 minutes at a time to gradually gain strength and coordination.

Note: A singer with an already developed head register will find the *belt mix* easier to learn than a singer with little or no head register. This is why it is so important to develop the head register. Also, you will find head register in almost every commercial/pop song. I begin every lesson with head register for both male and female students in all musical styles.

Chest Mix

A *belt mix* that has *more* firmness in the vocal folds, has an emphasis of chest color, and is closer to the *feel* and *sound* of chest register is what I refer to as *chest mix*.

Guidelines—chest mix
1. Use <u>more</u> focusing strength of the vocal folds.
2. Add chest color along with *mask* resonance.
3. Sing on a clear vowel.
4. Use good lower back support.

Head Mix

Guidelines—head mix
A *belt mix* that has *less* firmness in the vocal folds, that has an emphasis of mask and head colors and is closer to the *feel* and *sound* of *head* register is what I refer to as *head mix*.

1. Use <u>less</u> focusing strength of the vocal folds.
2. Stay in the mask head color and use less chest color.
3. Sing on a clear vowel.
4. Use good lower back support.

When adding chest color to the mask, feel the open throat space by thinking the sound, "uh," as in "under." "Lean" the sound against the chest bones, but do not necessarily add volume. Don't let the tongue press back in the throat. This technique allows you to sing higher notes in your belt mix without bringing full chest register too high.

Note: Exercises for belt mix also help strengthen the upper register of the head voice in females and falsetto in males.

The "Chest Lean"

Leaning the air pressure "against the chest" is a concept I read in a very interesting book on voice called, "How to Sing," published in 1902 by world renowned coloratura soprano, Lilli Lehmann. She says, "Besides giving steadiness, the pressure against the chest establishes the strength and the duration of the tone." I refer to this technique as the *chest lean,* which has made an obvious difference in my own voice and the voices of my students. The *chest lean* helps to enlarge the pharynx, strengthening the lower partials (component of tone) of the voice, giving substance and richness throughout the vocal range.

Helpful Hints

1. Stretch your range gradually. Work your mix notes higher and higher but never to the point of strain. There is a limit to how high any voice is capable of singing.
2. Just a few moments each day on the mix is recommended at first.
3. Use diaphragmatic vibrato on high, sustained notes.
4. Learn to "mark" your music, that is sing lightly when possible, especially if you have a long rehearsal.
5. Your mix is a vulnerable area and can become weak and raspy when there is vocal fatigue or if you have a cold. It's the first area to weaken.

Singing from the Mix into Head Register

You can practice singing from the mix into head register by using an ascending scale or a "siren-like slide" that begins on a low note in chest register, gradually decreasing the focusing strength of the vocal folds as you approach the mix and then releasing the folds even more as you go beyond the mix into head register. You can achieve a smooth blend throughout your voice with this exercise.

Exercises

(Singing Techniques CD, Track 28)

In the following exercises, use medium volume until your register transition is consistently smooth.

1. On the sound "*Hey*" or "nyaa" ("aa" as in c*at* [æ]), using good support and a clear tone, slide upwards on a siren-like tone, beginning in the lower register, and proceed slowly and smoothly through the passaggio into the upper register and then back down. As you feel yourself approaching your normal break area, lighten up the sound by relaxing your vocal folds slightly. The yawn will help relax the vocal folds. Be careful not to pull the tongue back in the throat. Keep your lower back muscles firm through the whole exercise.

2. For the female voice.
   Sing:

And for the male voice.
Sing:

As you move upward from the chest register through the passaggio into the mix, maintain mask resonance and a clear vowel throughout. Gradually release the focusing strength of the vocal folds as you widen the throat space (think "uh" as in "under") and add air pressure for a smooth transition.
Don't relax support on the downward slide.
There should be no obvious break in the voice. If you emphasize the mask resonance with a clear, well pronounced vowel, this will help keep the vocal folds focused throughout the exercise.

(Singing Techniques CD, Track 29)

3. Use this exercise for working on your blend (mixed register).
For the female voice:
Sing:

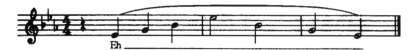

4. And for the male voice.
Sing:

Additional Exercises: Three Steps for Blending the Mix and Chest Register

1. Begin on a comfortably high note in your chest voice. Use a short, detached, staccato arpeggio downward and sing on "ow!" as in "ouch!" on each note. Maintain mask placement with an emphasis on the nasal resonance with very little chest resonance and not too loud.
Female voice sing:

Male voice sing:

2. Now sing the same arpeggio and connect the notes smoothly (legato). To avoid a glottal attack, approach the beginning of the vowel with a "silent h." The sound "Hey," works very well.

Female voice sing:

a (as in hat)_____

Male voice sing:

a (as in hat)____

3. Now sing the same exercise with four pulses of vibrato on each note.

Female voice sing:

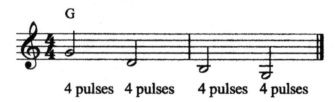

4 pulses   4 pulses   4 pulses 4 pulses

Male voice sing:

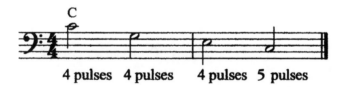

4 pulses   4 pulses   4 pulses   5 pulses

4. Now sing the same exercise with eight pulses of vibrato on each note.

Female voice sing:

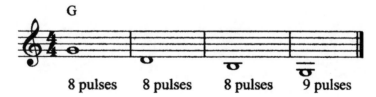

8 pulses   8 pulses   8 pulses   9 pulses

Male voice sing:

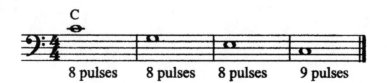

8 pulses   8 pulses   8 pulses   9 pulses

5. Here's another exercise for practicing blending your chest into your mix. Use "nya" [æ], as in "that":
Female voice sing:

nya —

Male voice sing:

nya —

6. Here's an exercise for practicing blending your chest into your mix using the Blues scale. Use "ay" [ɛi] as in day:
Female voice sing:

Male voice sing:

Try improvising your own melodies using your mix and then try it in a song!

CHAPTER TEN

The Lower Mix for the Female Singer

"Vocal Power is the consummate vocal method, giving the singer control of the instrument and versatility of style... the singer understands the whole spectrum of tools available in the singing voice." **Donna Hinds Sawyers**
Director: Studio Bella Voce,
Voice Faculty: North Harris College, Houston, TX
Vocal Power Associate, Houston, TX

(Singing Techniques CD, Track 30-32)

In classical or music theater vocal music, the soprano, mezzo soprano and contralto sing primarily in the upper register (head voice), using the lower mix for the lower tones, and pure lower register (chest voice) for dramatic effects. The soprano head voice, like falsetto for the male, becomes weaker in the lower range of the head voice. To compensate for this weakness, and in order to gain projection, the soprano must use her *lower mix* on these lower notes. The lower mix uses a light chest register with firmer vocal folds than head register, but less firm than full chest register. The lower mix matches the quality of the head register, giving substance to the lower notes, which would otherwise not be heard well (especially over an orchestra).

There is no *one* note where one register begins and the other ends. One register should blend into the other with no apparent or abrupt change in quality. The lower mix occurs approximately on the F above middle C and extends downward, into chest register for the lowest notes. The note range of the lower mix depends on the individual singer as well as the musical style. Lower mix can also be used above the staff for dramatic effect. The quality of the tones in the lower mix must match the upper register, unless it is the dramatic intent of the singer to sing contrasting qualities. Pure chest voice even above the staff may be used in some operetta for a "cabaret" style of singing.

Exercises

(Singing Techniques CD, Track 31)

In the following exercise, on the downward slide, add air pressure and focusing strength gradually as you increase chest resonance. Widen the throat space as you move into the lower mix. Maintain good support and mask resonance. Keep the tone focused and use a clear vowel. Practice on various vowels and work toward eliminating an obvious register break.

1. Using the vowel "ee" (as in *see*) [i]. Begin in upper register and move gradually into lower mix.

Sing:

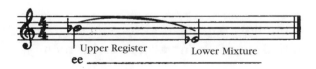

Upper Register   Lower Mixture

ee

2. Practice this exercise each time a half step lower until you are moving from lower mix into chest register.

(Singing Techniques CD, Track 32)

1. The following is a two part exercise that moves through lower mix smoothly to head voice and back. The first part stresses flexibility and the second part sustaining with vibrato. Be sure to sing on pitch in fast moving passages. Using the vowel "ee" (as in *see*) [i]. Begin in upper register and move gradually into lower mix.

Sing:

2. Repeat each of the above exercises using the following vowel sounds, beginning a half step lower each time.

"ah" as in f<u>a</u>r	[ɑ]
"uh" as in <u>mu</u>st	[ʌ]
"aw" as in l<u>aw</u>n	[ɔ]
"uu" as in l<u>oo</u>k	[ʊ]
"oo" as in s<u>oo</u>n	[u]

Helpful Hints

1. Begin with your jaw in a relaxed one finger width opening. Let the jaw lower on the higher notes and not before. If you lower the jaw all the way down before you get to the highest note, you will try to open even wider on the highest note, which will cause undue jaw tension. Don't hold your jaw in place. Good support will help to gain freedom in the jaw and tongue.

2. Use your "inner smile" to activate the mask resonance, but use your head resonance as a primary color. Too much mask for a soprano will sound non-classical.

3. The *chest lean* will help keep an even and warm sound throughout your range.

4. Keep your tongue relaxed and not tensed in the back of your throat. Keep the tongue free from the jaw for your pronunciation. Don't bring the tongue up and down with the jaw.

5. Always strive for beauty of tone, not how big and loud you can sing. Treat the high notes in an exercise as beautiful sounds, don't **accent** or **hit** them.

6. Feel your lower back support whether you are singing higher or lower.

7. Keep the lower mix low and the chest register even lower.

8. Use full chest voice only for dramatic effects.

9. Strengthen your head voice by bringing it as low as possible in exercises.

Keep singing and have fun!

SING!

NOTES

"I've been singing professionally for 20 years and Liz Howard has been invaluable in helping me keep my instrument finely tuned. Working with her has helped enhance my tone, increase my range and define my style."

Mavis
Singer/Songwriter for Cher's hit, "Take Me Home"

Vocal Style

"Liz's teaching is not a sing-song method. It strengthens, develops and enables you to reach new elements you thought you never could. It will give you techniques that last a life time."

Rachelle Dobins
15 year old soloist: Dodgers Stadium, NASCAR,
Staples Center, Ronald Reagan Presidential Library

SING!

NOTES

CHAPTER ELEVEN

Blues

"I sing with Elisabeth Howard's Vocal Power Method. It's easy! It's fun! It works! I recommend it to all who like to sing!"

Lalaine
Warner Recording Artist; "Miranda" in Disney's "Lizzie McGuire"

(Singing Style CD, Tracks 1-5)

Probably the greatest musical influence on all popular singing is the blues. In musical styles like the blues, rhythm and blues (R&B), rock and music with a blues flavor, there are vocal embellishments on the melodies called *licks* that use elements of the blues scale. These *licks* are emotional expressions of the singer. If you study the blues scale so that you can sing it up and down beginning on any note, you are well on your way to developing your ability to improvise in many vocal styles. In my studio, we use exercises on the blues scale as well as exercises on the major scale. We also use vocal exercises on the pentatonic scale because so many *licks* and improvisational melody lines include elements of both the blues and pentatonic scales. The pentatonic scale is discussed in Chapter 14, *Rock Style* (page 91).

Let your ear guide you, but you must let your ear absorb the sounds first. You can only sing what you can hear.

The Blues Scale

(Singing Style CD, Track 1)

The blues scale is built on the steps of the natural minor scale. One, three, four, sharp four, five, seven, eight. Be careful to sing the half steps on the way down in tune. Notice that on the way down the sharp four is spelled as a flat five.

Here is an example of the blues scale, beginning on C.

Sing:

If you are familiar with major and minor scales, you will notice that the intervals of the blues scale are different from the intervals of the major and minor scales. The intervals of the blues scale are:

minor 3rd	(1-1/2 steps)
Major 2nd	(whole step)
minor 2nd	(half step)
minor 2nd	(half step),
minor 3rd	(1-1/2 steps)
Major 2nd	(whole step)

Another way to think of the blues scale is to lower the 3rd, 5th and 7th notes of any major scale by a half step. These are called *blue notes*. The C major scale C - D - E - F - G - A - B - C can become a C blues scale C – E♭ - F - F♯ - G - B♭ - C. (On a descending line, the F♯ is written as a G♭). The lowered 5th, G♭, is really what gives a song a "blues feel."

Songs written in minor keys tend to be more melancholy. Since the blues scale is closely related to the minor scale and blues songs are written primarily with the notes of the blues scale, "singin' the Blues" often conveys a sad or melancholy theme.

Additional Blues Exercises

1. Here is the C blues scale. Sing "*doot*" on each note ascending and descending.

$$1-3^{\flat}-4-4^{\sharp}-5-7^{\flat}-8-(\sqrt{})-8-7^{\flat}-5-5^{\flat}-4-3^{\flat}-1$$

Notice that when ascending the C blues scale, we use a sharped 4th (F♯). When descending, we use a flatted 5th (G♭). The F♯ and G♭ are the same pitch spelled differently. Notes that sound the same, but are spelled differently are called *enharmonic equivalents*.

2. Sing the following blues melodies, slowly at first and then with a little more freedom and spontaneity. With repetition you will develop agility and freedom to express your music.

a)

b)

c)

d)

3. Choose other starting pitches and repeat the above exercises. Train yourself to sing the blues scale, ascending descending, beginning on any note. Make up your own blues melodies and have fun with it!

"Bent" Notes

Bending a note is heard in blues guitar playing, which is probably why blues singers who play guitar sing bent notes more easily. In country western style we hear bent notes played on other string instruments such as the violin, bass, mandolin and slide guitar. The piano can't bend notes, but a string instrument or a voice can.

You can give a song a blues feel by using elements of the blues scale for your own personal licks. A good way of getting a blues feel is by *bending* a note, which usually occurs on blue notes - the flat 3rd, 5th and 7th. *Bending* a note is when you sing or play slightly above or below the pitch to give a blues feel to the melody. You won't see bent notes written on sheet music. That's why listening to established blues singers and instrumentalists helps our ear to know where these bent notes happen.

Even though we are given the freedom to bend notes in singing the blues, pitch accuracy, which means good intonation and singing in tune, must be impeccable. Be especially accurate with the half steps in a descending line because there is a strong tendency to sing the pitches flat on the way down. In improvising with the blues scale, the ear must be trained to hear the appropriate use of blue notes. By listening to blues singers and instrumentalists, you will get the feel of where and when to use the *bent* or *blue note*.

I use the blues scale as exercises for my non-classical singers so that they can become flexible both musically and vocally. We use the blues scale up and down the entire vocal range, improvising melodies in head voice, chest voice, mix, high, low, loud and soft and with various vocal colors–head, nasal, mouth and chest. It becomes easy to hear how it applies to the performance of a song. We make it fun!

(Singing Style CD, Track 2)

Here's a phrase in the rhythm & blues style as it appears written in the sheet music.
Sing:

A singer familiar with the blues scale can transform that simple written phrase into this soulful expression.
Sing:

Here's another variation.
Sing:

(Singing Style CD, Track 3)

Here's a phrase in country style in its simple form, as it might appear in sheet music.
Sing:

Here it is again with some blue notes added on the second note in the second measure, the first note in the third measure and the third note in the third measure.

Sing:

Try this variation.

Sing:

(Singing Style CD, Track 4)

"Hidden" Notes

Here's a phrase from a rock ballad in its original form as written.

Sing:

If you play a recording of a commercial song (blues, R&B, country, rock, jazz) at a much slower tempo, you will notice *hidden* notes, that is, notes sung but not written on the printed page. These hidden notes play a major part in the style of any performing artist. The note usually occurs as either a whole or a half step below and before the written note. You may not be aware that singers use hidden notes (but they do), and the more you listen and sing along with the performer for style, the more obvious this will become to you. The hidden notes are what keep the song from sounding rigid or "straight".

Here's the above phrase again with added notes from the blues scale on "life" and "al-" and a blues lick on the second syllable of "al<u>right</u>."

Sing:

Here's another variation.

Sing:

(Singing Style CD, Track 5)

Play the following chord progression over and over and sing your own improvised melodies in the blues style. You may also use the accompaniment on the Style CD, Track 6. Experiment and have fun!

CHAPTER TWELVE

Improvisation

"Elisabeth Howard is living proof of the efficiency of her technique: Jumping from a rock voice to gospel, from opera to musical or R&B–all with disconcerting ease...the efficiency of this technique and the intelligence used allow us to discover in our own voices a music style. Finally, a technique in the service of the music!"

Martina Catella
Musician, Ethnomusicologist, Artistic Director (label Accords Croisés)
Paris, France

(Singing Style CD, Tracks 6-11)

When we speak of improvisation in singing, it refers to taking an established melody and making up our own variations of the melodies and rhythms. You can use the same words or make up word syllables, as is done in jazz *scatting*. You can alter the original melody by using added notes, blue notes and licks and by choosing other melodies that resemble the original melody. You can change rhythms by using syncopations. You can change the phrasing by using *back phrasing* and *anticipation.* (See Chapter 21, *Jazz* on page 113).

The ability to improvise is a sign of a well trained singer and musician. These improvised passages are spontaneous when first sung, but become so well rehearsed and performed so often, that they actually become part of the performance each and every time, with little variation.

It is important for the singer to always be aware of the accompanying chord progression when improvising. The notes of an improvised melody must be harmonically compatible with the notes in the chord progression. For example, if the chord is an F chord, F-A-C, and you sing F#, A# or C#, you will sing notes that *clash (dissonant)* with the accompanying chord.

Learn an Instrument

Being able to play the basics on piano or guitar is a tremendous asset to a singer, not only for self-accompaniment, but for developing musicianship. Your ear, mind, fingers and eyes are involved in playing an instrument. The more senses that are involved, the better you will be as a singer and a musician.

A good practice exercise is to sing along with an instrumental recording without the vocal(s), first on the original tune, then singing variations of the original melody. Use syllables like "doot," rather than words, so that you can clearly hear your melody line against the chord progressions.

Guidelines

1. The verse is a repeating section of the same music with different lyrics each time the section repeats. The verse continues the story line. You can improvise on the repeat of the verse.

2. You can also improvise on the repeat of the chorus. The chorus is a section of the same music with the same lyric between the verses. The chorus emphasizes the message of the song and usually contains the "hook." A "hook" is a repeating, catchy and memorable phrase in a song.

3. You can improvise on instrumental introductions to a song.
4. You can improvise on the *breaks*. A break is an instrumental interlude in a song where the instruments improvise and the singer becomes a part of the musical ensemble.
5. You can improvise on repeat and fade endings. Repeat and fade endings are at the end of a song where a phrase is repeated, gradually becoming softer and softer and eventually fades out. The "fade out" is done by the recording engineer.

(Singing Style CD, Track 6)

Here's a phrase as it might be sung in country style as written.

Here it is again with added melody notes.

Sing:

Here's another variation with licks on "more" and "day".

Sing:

(Singing Style CD, Track 7)

Here's another country phrase in its simple form.

Sing:

Here it is again with added melody notes on the word "talkin.'" Notice how this lick brings out the country flavor of the phrase.

Sing:

Here's another way to sing the same phrase.

Sing:

Practice all of these phrases slowly at first, then up to tempo.

(Singing Style CD, Track 8)

Here's a phrase in the R&B or "soul" style without improvisation.

Sing:

Here it is again with some style, using added melody notes. Notice the lick on the word "cry," which increases the emotional impact.

Sing:

Here's another way to sing that phrase with more variation.

Sing:

(Singing Style CD, Track 9)

Here's another R&B phrase in its simple form without embellishments.

Sing:

Here it is again with a lick on the word, "man."
Sing:

Try this variation.
Sing:

(Singing Style CD, Track 10)

Here's a phrase in rock style, in its simple form.
Sing:

Here's another way to sing that phrase with added melody notes for embellishment.
Sing:

Here's another variation of the same phrase.
Sing:

(Singing Style CD, Track 11)

Here's another phrase from a rock ballad, as written.
Sing:

Now, with added melody notes.
Sing:

Try this variation.
Sing:

CHAPTER THIRTEEN

Vocal Colors and Dynamics in Songs

*"My studies with Elisabeth gave me the ability to perform reper-
toire many thought I was too young to perform. Top vocal coaches
I studied with during my lessons with Elisabeth were surprised by
my ability to handle these physically challenging pieces with ease.
It was due to the technique Elisabeth taught me."*

Alexandra Lee
Winner, Los Angeles Music Center Spotlight Award
Juilliard student

(Singing Style CD, Tracks 12-15)

Your ability to control the variations in resonance, color and volume can make a world of
difference in your personal singing style. Just as the painter has greater freedom of choice
by having more colors on his or her palate, you, the singing artist, have greater freedom to
express yourself in a more exciting and emotional way by using the colors on your palette (or
should we say palate?). With your vocal skills, you can use your colors, mixing and blending
them to enrich your interpretation of a song.

We have explored our four vocal colors, *head, nasal, mouth* and *chest* in Chapter 7 (page 55),
Good Vibrations! Vocal Colors, Resonance. Let's see how they work in song phrases in the
following exercises.

Resonance and Vocal Color Exercises

(Singing Style CD, Track 12)

1. In this phrase, emphasize chest color all the way through without variation.
   Sing:

2. Emphasize head color all the way through without variation. (It will be much softer.)
   Sing:

(Singing Style CD, Track 13)

3. Begin with chest color moving to head color and back to chest color by the end
   of the phrase.
   Sing:

SING!

Dynamics

We explored our control of dynamics in Chapter 5 (page 37). Crescendo and decrescendo are tools of expression in singing. Let's see how dynamics work in song phrases in the following exercises.

Volume and Resonance Exercises

(Singing Style CD, Track 14)

1. Begin in chest color with greater volume and move smoothly with a decrescendo into head color.
   Sing:

2. Begin at low volume, crescendo to medium volume and decrescendo to soft by the end of the phrase.
   Sing:

(Singing Style CD, Track 15)

3. Sing the following phrase softly with a mouth/nasal resonance without variation.
   Sing:

4. Now use greater volume in chest color without variation.
   Sing:

5. Now begin softly with mouth/nasal resonance, crescendo with chest color and decrescendo into head color.

Sing:

1. Exercise your voice daily with the Vocal Power *Sing-Aerobics* CD that accompanies this book.

2. Expand your vocal technique and style even further by using the *Style* and *Super Vocals* CD that accompanies this book.

3. Learn to read music, improve your sight-reading and your musical ear, and learn to sing harmony with the *ABC's of Vocal Harmony* book and four CDs by Elisabeth Howard. For ordering information, go to our website: www.vocalpowerinc.com

SING!

NOTES

CHAPTER FOURTEEN

Rock Style

"Vocal Power enabled me to become a singer with power, presence and (most importantly) amazing technique."

Sarah Hudson
S Curve EMI Recording Artist

(Singing Style CD, Tracks 16-18)

The Pentatonic Scale

The pentatonic scale is prevalent in all of rock music, including hard rock, soft rock, jazz rock, rock-a-billy, classical rock, heavy metal, rock 'n' roll, southern rock and folk rock. Entire songs are often built on this scale.

Note: In classical music, the Impressionist composers of the late 19th century and early 20th century, such as Claude Debussy, Gabriel Fauré and Maurice Ravel, used the pentatonic scale in much of their music.

(Singing Style CD, Track 16)

As the name "pentatonic" suggests, "penta," means "5" and the pentatonic scale is a 5 note scale. If you play only the 5 black notes on the piano, you will be playing the notes of a pentatonic scale.

(Singing Style CD, Track 17)

D♭ - E♭ - G♭ - A♭ - B♭

Pentatonic Exercises

Here are two examples of pentatonic scales.
Sing:

C   D   E   G   A   G♭ A♭ B♭ D♭ E♭

1. Here's a melody using the pentatonic scale.
Sing:

C   D   E   G   A   C   A   G   E   D   C

(Singing Style CD, Track 18)

2. Here's a rock phrase as written, using the pentatonic scale.
   Sing:

   Here it is with a blue note on the word "baby":
   Sing:

3. Practice improvising melodies using only the notes of the pentatonic scale. Feel
   free to use elements of both the blues and pentatonic scales to add dimension
   and expression to your rock style.

"Pop Coloratura"

For fast and clean *licks* in commercial/pop singing, I use the same technique as I use for my classical coloratura singing. I call it "*pop coloratura*." It's done with the articulation of the vocal folds and is similar to the vocal fold flutter, only that several different notes are sung in fast succession. Your support must be kept steady throughout. You can use any vocal color and dynamic you wish–and in any part of your range.

"Pop coloratura" technique keeps you from sliding around on licks. Even though professional singers sound like it is natural and they were born with the ability to sing licks, it is because these singers listened hard and studied the singing of professionals who came before them. Listening and repeating over and over again is the best way of accomplishing fast clean, on pitch licks. Listen to some of the great blues and R&B singers. Try to hear the exact notes and repeat what you hear. Licks are built on exact notes, no matter how free and spontaneous they sound. Record yourself and listen back to your singing. Sometimes what we hear as we are singing is not accurate, but the recording tells us the truth. Play a simple chord and see how many variations you can come up with using the pentatonic scale.

Play with it! Have fun!

CHAPTER FIFTEEN

Pronunciation In Song

"Liz' Vocal Power Method did not only teach me how to increase the power and the range of my voice but also enabled me to feel at home in numerous vocal styles–be it pop, rock, musicals or opera. She is a truly unique and gifted teacher and I recommend her technique to anyone who is serious about this business."

Maik Lohse
Chris in "Miss Saigon" USA National Tour and Germany

(Singing Style CD, Track 19-24)

We have worked on power and projection, but it is the pronunciation of words that makes us understood. Words are sustained on vowel sounds. The way a word is written may have little to do with the way it is actually pronounced. For example, what vowel sound would you sustain on the word, "cry?" The vowel sound to be sustained is "ah" as in f**a**r [ɑ]. The second sound is "ih" as in s**i**t   [ɪ]. This is a diphthong, two vowel sounds one after the other. As we learned in Chapter 4 (page 29), on pronunciation in the Vocal Technique section, the first vowel sound is the one we sustain longer and the second vowel sound is sustained for a shorter duration. We must be very clear what vowel sounds we are sustaining, for two reasons:

1. When we sing a clear, open vowel sound, the vocal folds focus better, which in turn helps the air pressure to balance with the vocal fold adduction, giving us more control of our vibrato.
2. When we sing a clear, open vowel, the word is more easily understood by our audience.

Since there are so many long and high sustained notes in classical music, if your vowels are unclear, one word could be mistaken for another. For example, if you were sustaining the word, "father," you would sustain the "ah" f[ɑ]. If you pronounce the f[ɑ] like f[ʌ] as in "f**u**n," you won't be understood. We never want our audience to have to strain to understand what we are saying.

In music theater, the pronunciation has to fit the character. Characters can range from a very British character, such as Henry Higgins, in "My Fair Lady," to the very New York, Mimi, in "Rent." In rhythm & blues style, we wouldn't sing with a British accent. We would use pronunciation closer to the blues style of pronunciation.

In country western style, it depends how far back in time we go. If we go back to bluegrass, in the early part of the 20th century, in the southern USA, then the pronunciation has to reflect the way words were pronounced in that time and place. Otherwise it doesn't sound like bluegrass. In the late 20th century, singers began using less country pronunciation and "crossed over" into the "middle of the road" (MOR) "easy listening" category. Some country western singers continue the tradition and retain the country western pronunciation. In country western singing, you really can't separate the dialect from the pronunciation. There are expressions that are used in the southern USA that are not typical in the North. These expressions would sound out of place with a New York accent. And what is a New York accent?

Up state Rochester, New York, pronunciation sounds nothing like the pronunciation in the Bronx, New York. And if you listen carefully, the Bronx accent is different from Brooklyn accent in New York. But this is the beauty of language. Pronunciation must be authentic to the style of singing.

Let's listen to examples of how we would analyze the authenticity of singing in country western style.

(Singing Style CD, Track 19)

Without "country" pronunciation,
Sing:

With "country" pronunciation,
Sing:

Ah feel so praahoud when Ahm with yeeoo

Notice in the second example the broadening of the vowel sound in the word "I" and "proud" and the "ee" sound in the word "you."

(Singing Style CD, Tracks 20-21)

Here's a rhythm & blues phrase, first with standard diction.
Sing:

Now, with a more "authentic" R&B pronunciation...
Sing:

Don'cha know you always make me smaahl.

(Singing Style CD, Track 22)

Rock singers tend to use a conversational pronunciation which may or may not include regional or foreign accents. The English accent became part of the American rock sound when groups like the Beatles came on the scene.

Rock singers also tend to use very little vibrato on sustained tones. They also tend to use percussive, high-intensity vocal sounds, and often a rough and raspy vocal quality.

(Singing Style CD, Track 23)

Note: Avoid too much high, loud and raspy singing. You can damage your voice.

(Singing Style CD, Track 24)

Compare these two phrases.
Sing:

Sing:

Maah laahfs reflected in your aahs

In the first example, the speech pattern and phrasing were too precise and the vibrato too obvious. In the second example, the diction was closer to natural speech, phrasing more creative and the vibrato less obvious.

Classical and music theater singers generally use standard American stage diction, unless the character they are playing calls for a dialect.

For a more in-depth study of standard stage diction, refer to:

American Diction for Singers, Book and 2 CDs by Geoffrey G. Forward, published and distributed by Alfred Publishing, Inc.; and
PowerSpeech, Book and 2CDs by Geoffrey G. Forward.

For more information on these books go to www.vocalpowerinc.com

SING!

NOTES

CHAPTER SIXTEEN

Phrasing

"Elisabeth Howard is human dynamo-full of boundless energy and heart. She has enough successful students and former students to populate several Broadway shows, an entire city of cabaret theaters and a few opera houses to boot! She is living proof that her techniques work."

Henry Price
Director, Flora Thornton Opera Program, Pepperdine University

(Singing Style CD, Track 25-37)

Phrasing refers to the way in which you group and emphasize the lyrics of a song to fit your personal style and emotional expression. In commercial/pop music, you have freedom to vary your phrasing. The Broadway or classical singer is expected to adhere more closely to the phrasing written by the composer.

Phrasing Guidelines

1. Speak the words first. By speaking the words, you will discover how you would say the phrase naturally. Notice which words you emphasize.
2. In an acting monologue, we use a *sub text*. On a separate sheet of paper, write your own emotions under each phrase. For example, if the words are, "I feel a song comin' on," you might write under the words, "I feel so happy, I want to sing because I have a new love in my life." Be specific - who is this new love? What are the important words in that phrase? "I," "feel," "song," "comin'," "on." The word, "a," is not an important word to emphasize.

For Commercial/Pop Singers

1. When learning a new song, first sing the phrases as written on the page, both melody and rhythms, so that you have a basis from which to work out your own variations.
2. Make sure that you establish the original tune before you improvise your own.
3. You are not obliged to hold a word that is written to be held. You may choose another word if it makes more sense to you.
4. If a word occurs on a downbeat, you have a choice of *anticipating*, that is, singing the word before the downbeat, or *back phrasing*, singing the word after the downbeat. (See chapter 21, *Jazz* on page 113.)
5. You can sing a phrase in less time than is indicated on the sheet music and make up for it by stretching out the following phrase and visa versa. Just don't stray too far from the original.
6. Always be aware of the chord changes accompanying the melody. Too much flexibility in the phrasing may cause you to sound off pitch. The notes of your melody must be compatible with the underlying chords of the accompaniment.

SING!

Phrasing Exercises

The following examples illustrate how you can take an original melody and by re-phrasing, you can create a more natural and professional result.

Country western style with the original phrasing, as written,

Sing:

Re-phrased to express more feeling.

Sing:

Now let's take the lyric from that country phrase and re-set it in rhythm & blues style with the original phrasing and rhythm, as written.

Sing:

Re-phrased for more expressiveness and truth.

Sing:

Repeated Phrases

When a phrase repeats several times in a song, you can build emotional excitement by improvising increasingly elaborate melodies each time you sing that phrase.

Here's the same phrase as you might sing it the second time it occurs in the song.

Sing:

Here it is again as it might be sung the third time
Sing:

(Singing Style CD, Track 29)

Here's an accompaniment for that phrase for you to practice with. Sing it three times in a row. Make up your own variations.

(Singing Style CD, Track 30)

Here's the same lyric with the original rhythm using a different melody set in rock style.
Sing:

Here it is again with more inventive phrasing to express more feeling.
Sing:

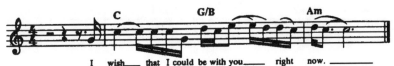

Here it is again as it might be sung the second time in the song.
Sing:

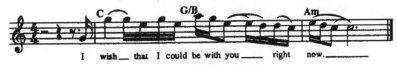

And the third time:
Sing:

(Singing Style CD, Track 31)

Use this chord progression to practice your own variations.

SING!

(Singing Style CD, Track 32)

Here are a couple of phrases in blues style, as written.
Sing:

Here it is again with an improvisational variation.
Sing:

(Singing Style CD, Track 33)

Use this accompaniment to practice your improvisational skills.

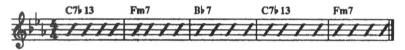

(Singing Style CD, Track 34)

Let's go country! Here's a country phrase, first as written, followed by improvisations on the melody.
Sing:

Here's a variation with improvisational licks.
Sing:

(Singing Style CD, Track 35)

Use the same accompaniment to practice your own licks.

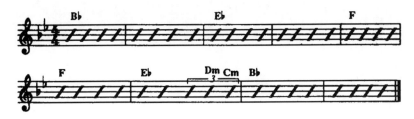

(Singing Style CD, Track 36)

Let's rock! Here's the original phrase as written.
Sing:

Try this improvisational treatment of the same phrase.
Sing:

(Singing Style CD, Track 37)

Repeat the same accompaniment five times in a row to develop your own improvisational skills and explore new choices that are more personal and more expressive.

SING!

NOTES

CHAPTER SEVENTEEN

Personal Style

"To paraphrase, 'Liz Howard has forgotten more than most people will ever know about the human voice.' She has an excellent command over the instrument and is expert at imparting her special knowledge about technique."

Harriet Schock
Platinum/Gold Songwriter ("Ain't No Way To Treat A Lady")
Recording Artist/Songwriting Teacher, Los Angeles, California

In every genre of vocal music, there is an accepted standard of interpretation of the music. The only way to acquire the appropriate style in your own voice is to listen, analyze and absorb what you hear. Developing your own personal style or changing to a new style involves using your vocal technique to suit the style. Elements of style include variations in registers, pronunciation, vocal coloration, vibrato and phrasing. Remember, your ear guides your voice, and your technique gives you the ability to sing what you hear.

Developing Personal Style

The following are guidelines that have been used throughout time by the great artists in every field, from jazz to classical. Studying the successful artists that have made their mark is the only way we can develop our own style. If we were born and isolated on a desert island, would we naturally know the difference between opera and country western style?

Guidelines

1. Choose the genre of music that you like.
2. Choose a recording of a song by an artist you admire in a comfortable key for your voice.
3. Carefully listen to one phrase at a time. Study the phrasing, licks, colors, "creaky" door, "throat cry," "throat laugh," "Back L," pronunciation, dynamics and vibrato. Sing one phrase at a time after the singer, copying exactly what the singer did.
4. After you have mastered the song to the best of your ability, go on to another song.
5. Don't use the same artist for more than two or three songs in succession. Choose other artists in the same genre and study their styles. Believe it or not, your own style will naturally evolve. You will automatically pick up and retain those qualities which suit your voice and personality and leave behind those characteristics that don't.
6. Choose a very simple song, perhaps a folk song, and sing it your own way. Use your registers, vocal colors, pronunciation, dynamics and vibrato as tools of expression. Be creative in your phrasing and use licks if appropriate to the style.

Negative feedback

People who say, "I can't carry a tune in a bucket" are usually those who as children were told by a teacher or parent to "Be quiet," or to "Just mouthe the words." Negative feedback at an early age, especially from an authority figure, can affect self confidence, not only in singing but in life, since the voice is an expression of who we are.

I believe that it is never too early or too late to learn how to sing beautifully. With solid technique, every voice can be beautiful!

CHAPTER EIGHTEEN

Music Theater

"With the Vocal Power Method you develop a healthy, strong, controlled voice. This technique has given me the confidence to sing in any vocal situation. I recommend it to beginners and progessionals as well."

Jennie Kwan
"Ave Q," Las Vegas; TV's "California Dreams;" "Miss Saigon;"
"Nobody's Angel;" Vocal Power Associate, Los Angeles, CA

(Singing Style CD, Track 38-39)

Let's take a look at some of the vocal characteristics of music theater. We will first begin with traditional music theater style, then look at music theater with an opera influence and then the commercial/pop style musical.

1. The Broadway singer plays a specific character in a musical play. Choice of speech pattern and vocal quality depend not only on his or her own understanding of the character, but are also guided by the author and director and the actors own understanding of the character.

2. In traditional music theater, the composer and lyricist have set down the song to be sung the way it appears on the sheet music. Then a precedent is set by the original cast member who has coached with the music director and stage director of the show. The audience will expect to hear a similar interpretation of the role each time with little variation in tempo, dynamics and interpretation. The stage director, composer and/or music director will usually have the final word on these elements.

3. In pop style music theater, there is a little more flexibility allowed the original cast, which then sets a precedent for following performers.

4. Key changes of a song are not changed to suit the vocal range of the performer in music theater. All future performers of that role must sing the song in the original key. This is because when a key is changed from the original, it involves changing the key for all the instruments in the orchestra. This can be quite expensive. The exception is when a well known "star" takes over the role.

Traditional Music Theater Examples

"Carousel," by Richard Rodgers and Oscar Hammerstein
"The King and I," by Richard Rodgers and Oscar Hammerstein
"The Sound of Music," by Richard Rodgers and Oscar Hammerstein
"Oklahoma!" by Richard Rodgers and Oscar Hammerstein
"South Pacific," by Richard Rodgers and Oscar Hammerstein
"Show Boat," by Jerome Kern and Oscar Hammerstein
"My Fair Lady," by Alan Jay Lerner and Frederick Loewe
"Camelot," by Alan Jay Lerner and Frederick Loewe
"Funny Girl," by Jule Styne and Bob Merrill
"Fiddler on the Roof," by Jerry Bock, Sheldon Harnick and Joseph Stein

"Annie Get Your Gun," by Irving Berlin, Herbert and Dorothy Fields
"The Phantom of The Opera," by Andrew Lloyd Webber, Charles Hart and Richard Stilgoe
"The Producers," by Mel Brooks and Thomas Meehan
"Thoroughly Modern Millie," by Richard Morris and Dick Scanlan, with additional material by Jeanine Tesori.

Traditional Music Theater and Opera combined

Musicals Performed as Opera

"Candide," by Leonard Bernstein
"Porgy and Bess," by George Gershwin
"Street Scene," by Kurt Weill
"Sweeney Todd," by Stephen Sondheim

Pop Style (Commercial) Music Theater Examples

"Hair," by Gerome Ragni, James Rado and Galt MacDermott
"Jesus Christ Superstar," by Andrew Lloyd Webber and Tim Rice
"Tommy," by Pete Townshend and Des McAnuff
"Dreamgirls," by Tom Eyen and Henry Krieger
"Grease," by Warren Casey and Jim Jacobs
"Cats," by Andrew Lloyd Webber and T. S. Eliot
"Miss Saigon," by Claude-Michel Schonberg, Richard Maltby Jr., and Alain Boublil
"The Lion King," by Elton John and Tim Rice
"Aida," by Elton John and Tim Rice
"Jekyll and Hyde," by Frank Wildhorn and Leslie Bricusse
"Hair Spray," by Mark O'Donell, Thomas Meehan, Marc Shaiman and Scott Wittman
"The Life," by Cy Coleman, Ira Gasman and David Newman
"Mama Mia," featuring the music of the rock group "Abba"

Be Prepared For Auditions - Females

For auditions, you will usually be asked to prepare a ballad and an up-tempo song. Tailor your audition selections to fit the style of the show. Many casting people specify that they do not want to hear a song from the show they are casting, but will ask for songs in the style of that show. Sometimes they will be specific: Sing an R&B ballad. Sing a rock song. Often they will ask for a main stream, pop style song, not from a musical if the show is in pop style.

Females need to develop a strong chest and head voice, a lower mix and a belt mix. *There are six different belt styles and three soprano styles.* My advice is to find your "best voice" in the style you feel most comfortable singing and concentrate on being the best you can be in that style. It's better to be outstanding in one style, than mediocre in several styles. But make sure you also have several styles ready for auditions, just in case. Some singers manage to perfect several styles. It depends on how much time one can devote to practice.

Styles most required at auditions – Females

Six female belt styles:

1. *Traditional belt* - example: "A Little Brains, a Little Talent," from "Damn Yankees," by Richard Adler and Jerry Ross.
2. *Torch song belt* - example: "And the World Goes Round," from "And the World Goes Round," featuring the music of John Kander and Fred Ebb.
3. *Soprano belt* - example: "Gimme, Gimme," from "Thoroughly Modern Millie," by Richard Morris and Dick Scanlan.
4. *Rock belt* - example: "Out Tonight," from "Rent," by Jonathan Larson.
5. *Rhythm & Blues belt* - example: "And I Am Telling You," from "Dreamgirls," by Tom Eyen and Henry Krieger.
6. *Character belt* - example: "Good Morning Baltimore," from "Hair Spray," by Mark Shaiman, Thomans Meehan, Mark O'Donnell and Scott Wittman.

Three soprano styles

1. *Operatic soprano* - example: "Climb Every Mountain," from "The Sound of Music," by Richard Rodgers and Oscar Hammerstein.
2. *Light belt soprano* - example: "Wouldn't it be Loverly," from "My Fair Lady," by Alan Jay Lerner and Frederick Loewe.
3. *Light soprano* - example: "Think of Me," from "The Phantom of the Opera," by Andrew Lloyd Webber, Charles Hart and Richard Stilgoe.

Be Prepared For Auditions - Males

For music theater auditions, male performers are also required to prepare songs in various styles, depending on the musical style of the show. For example, you will usually be asked to prepare a ballad and an up-tempo song. Tailor your selections to the style of the show. Male singers should develop a *chest*, *head* (falsetto) and *belt mix*. They should be prepared with at least four styles of singing. As I stated to the female performers, my advice is to find your "best voice" in the style you feel most comfortable singing and concentrate on being the best you can be in that style. But make sure you also have other styles ready for auditions. It's better to be outstanding in one style, than mediocre in several styles.

Styles most required at auditions – Males

1. *Romantic traditional* (baritone) - example: "If Ever I Would Leave you," from "Camelot," by Alan Jay Lerner and Frederick Loewe
2. *Romantic traditional* (tenor) - example: "Younger Than Spring Time," from "South Pacific," by Richard Rodgers and Oscar Hammerstein, II.
3. *Rock* (tenor) - example: "I Only Want to Say," from "Jesus Christ Superstar," by Andrew Lloyd Webber and Tim Rice.
4. *Rock* (tenor, high baritone) - example: "Pin Ball Wizard," from " Tommy," by Pete Townshend and Des McAnuff.
5. *R&B* (baritone) - example: "A Piece of the Action," from the show, "The Life," by Cy Coleman and Ira Gasman.
6. *R&B* (tenor) - example: "On the Deck of a Spanish Ship," from the New York workshop production of "Songs For a New World," by Jason Robert Brown.

7. *Character* (baritone) - example: "The King of Broadway," from "The Producers," by Mel Brooks.
8. *Character* (tenor) - example: "Closed For Renovation," from "Little Shop of Horrors," by Howard Ashman and Ira Gasman.

In conclusion

We must remember the importance of a healthy vocal technique to withstand the challenges of singing some roles in commercial/pop music theater, especially if one is not used to singing commercial/pop music. Also, what you hear on a recording isn't always healthy singing. This is why singers should seek the guidance of a voice teacher who knows the style of the music when they are working on their roles in a show or preparing for an audition.

Sometimes you have to weigh the benefits of doing a show that may have a detrimental effect on your voice. If your technique is not solid, you may be wise not to do the show, especially if you are performing in a long run of a show or on tour, away from your teacher who knows your voice and can guide you. We must always be vigilant when it comes to our precious instrument, our voice. We must use safe vocal techniques that will still produce the dramatic effects that the role requires.

The vocal demands in music theater are tremendous. If you are planning to become a professional performer you should consider being prepared in several singing styles. Be prepared with audition songs that fit the style of the show. One day, you may be asked to sing a Puccini aria and the next day, a Rolling Stones song!

Sing and Have Fun!

(Singing Style CD, Tracks 38-39)

You can hear some music theater examples on the Singing Style CD, Tracks 38-39.

Music Theater Artists

Women

Julie Andrews, Joan Diener, Bernadette Peters, Ethel Merman, Sutton Foster, Idina Menzel, Kristin Chenoweth, Patti Lupone, Jeanette MacDonald, Betty Buckley, Karen Morrow, Nancy Dussault, Liza Minnelli, Judy Garland, Linda Eder, Paige O'Hara, Sarah Brightman, Mary Martin, Barbara Cook, Jennifer Holiday, Rita Gardner, Susan Watson, Joanna Gleason, Carol Channing, Barbara Harris, Pearl Bailey.

Men

Alfred Drake, John Raitt, Douglas Sills, Robert Preston, Robert Goulet, Rex Harrison, Richard Kiley, Brian Stokes Mitchell, Jerry Orbach, Hugh Jackman, Harve Presnell, Mandy Patinkin, John Cullum, Len Cariou, Zero Mostel, Colm Wilkinson, Michael Crawford, Ezio Pinza, Harvey Fierstein, Tom Aldredge, Nathan Lane, Nelson Eddy, Howard Keel, Mathew Broderick.

CHAPTER NINETEEN

More on the Blues

"Liz Howard has widened my vocal range and improved my singing technique, giving me the freedom to sing with more confidence and style. After working with Liz, I am now singing on Broadway in 'Ave. Q'!"

Minglie Chen
"Ave. Q" on Broadway, "Miss Saigon" National Tour and Germany,
Jasmine in Disneyland's "Aladdin"

"And then they nursed it, rehearsed it and gave out the news that the Southland gave "Birth to the Blues."
Lyric by B.G. De Sylva and Lew Brown; Music by Ray Henderson

"The blue note is endemic in jazz, blues and gospel, and has settled in every corner of American music from Tin Pan Alley to Nashville and from symphonies to new wave rock. Yet it is invisible in Western musicology: a microtone - a wavering pitch between, say, a third and a flat third - can't be notated. In recent years, musicologists have comforted themselves by redefining the blue note as a flat third, flat fifth, and flat seventh. Even so, the blue note remains elusive, appreciable only in relation to another note. But we know it when we hear it, and we hear it constantly. The black performers were raised on it and the white performers were transformed by it."

– Excerpt from "Riding on a Blue Note"- Jazz and American Pop, by Gary Giddins.

"Singing the blues, and this is particularly true of the Delta's Deep blues, involves very precise manipulation of vocal timbre, very subtle variations in timing and inflection, and very fine gradations in pitch."

– Excerpt from" Deep Blues," by Robert Palmer.

Blues legend Billie Holiday wrote, "I can't stand to sing the same song the same way two nights in succession... If you can, then it ain't music, it's close order drill or yodeling or something, not music."

– Excerpt from "Riding on a Blue Note," by Gary Giddins.

Mississippi Delta Style: Developed out of *call and response* field songs on the plantation. The Mississippi Delta Style of Blues is the sound of one man with heart rending vocals and virtuoso fretwork on his guitar, telling of hard times. Often, songs were based on one chord. Tommy Johnson, Muddy Waters and Howlin' Wolf represent Mississippi Delta Blues singers.

"Singing the blues —and this is particularly true of the Delta's deep blues—involves very precise manipulations of vocal timbre, very subtle variations in timing and inflection, very fine gradations in pitch. When Muddy (Muddy Waters) sings, he screws up the side of his face and constantly readjusts the shape (and thus the resonating capacity) of his mouth cavity, all in order to get different, precisely calibrated vocal sounds, from the purest falsetto to deep, quivering moans, to a grainy, vibrato-heavy rasp."

– Excerpt from"Deep Blues," by Robert Palmer.

SING!

New Orleans Blues: Adds the high spirits of Dixieland Jazz, mixes calypso, creole and ragtime into a style all its own. New Orleans Blues is exemplified in the music of Professor Longhair, a boogie-woogie pianist with a croaking - yodeling voice and is often spoken of as the foundation for New Orleans Rock and Roll and Rhythm and Blues. He was also said to have been the mentor of Fats Domino and Huey Smith. Professor Longhair's rumba rhythms influenced the styles of Ruth Brown, the Coasters and the Drifters.

Texas Blues: Blends shuffle beat, jazz, country and cajun into a laid-back swinging style. Noted artists are Freddie King, and Lightnin' Hopkins.

The Chicago Blues: Adapted the deep Delta Blues, added drums and a strutting bass to plugged in guitars and were the foundation for 1960's rock and soul. The Rolling Stones took their name from Muddy Waters song, "Rollin' Stone." Muddy Waters left the Delta and moved to Chicago in search of work. Eventually, Muddy and his band were the unquestioned leaders of the "Chicago Blues Pack" in the late 1940's and early 1950's. Others were B.B King and Hound Dog Taylor.

For a fascinating journey on the history of the blues I recommend "Deep Blues," by Robert Palmer (Penguin Press) and "Ridin' on a Blue Note," by Gary Giddins (Oxford University Press)

Stylistic Characteristics

1. Resonance - nasal resonance is typical. *Creaky door* and *Back L* is typical.
2. Register Breaks - the register break is typical.
3. Blues Licks and bent notes are used freely and expressively throughout blues songs.
4. Vibrato - straight tone, diaphragmatic vibrato, throat vibrato, flutter vibrato. Shimmering vibrato is used, but rarely.
5. "Throat cry and throat laugh" are typical.
6. Pronunciation - Colloquial, every day speech, reflecting the pronunciation of the early 20th Century in southern states of the United States.

Blues Artists

Robert Johnson, Johnny Lang, Charley Patton, Howlin' Wolf, John Lee Hooker, Professor Longhair, Muddy Waters, Bobby "Blues" Bland, Lightnin' Hopkins, B. B. King, Hound Dog Taylor, Big Bill Broonzy, Mamie Smith, Ethel Waters, Bessie Smith, Ruth Brown, Etta James, Dinah Washington, Jimmy Rogers, Little Walter, Robert Nighthawk, Eddie Boyd, Betty Carter, Stevie Ray Vaughn and Double Trouble, Koko Taylor, Ike Turner, Son Seals, James Cotton, Albert Collins, Johnny Copeland, Bonnie Raitt, Eric Clapton, Dr. John, Keb Mo', Kim Wilson, Maria Muldaur, Jimmie Vaughn, Ray Charles, Joe Williams, Susan Tedeschi, Elmore James, Jimmy Reed, Albert King, Buddy Guy, Charlie Musselwhite and Billie Holiday.

CHAPTER TWENTY

Rhythm & Blues

"Elisabeth Howard's technique has given me the power and consistency needed in order to obtain and sustain a career in the professional world of singing"

Nicole Pryor
Disneyworld's "American Vybe," Sarah in "Ragtime,"
Las Vegas' "Phantom of the Opera," "California Dreaming"

Rhythm & Blues, typically referred to as "R&B" or "soul," was a natural outgrowth of blues. The music is passionate. The lyrics are passionate. The voices are passionate. Expressing passion takes many forms. When we speak, we emphasize words by speaking them louder or even by speaking very softly on a word. We cry, we laugh, we giggle, we moan. All these emotions are expressed when we speak and need to be expressed when we sing. The study and singing of rhythm & blues, soul and gospel could benefit any singer in any style, including classical.

Vocal characteristics of Rhythm & Blues:

Resonance

1. In R&B there are abrupt changes from one vocal color to another within the same phrase or even on the same note.
2. The *creaky door* sound is typically used on words beginning with vowels. For example: I always think about us.
3. Many R&B singers use the *Back L*. A good example of the "Back L" can be heard in the singing of pop/R&B artist, Cristina Aguilera, for example, in the song, "Fighter," from her album, "Stripped."

Registers

1. Head voice for female and male singer falsetto is typical. Peabo Bryson is a good example of an R&B artist who uses falsetto in much of his singing.
2. The belt mix is used on the higher notes to match the chest voice.
3. There are abrupt changes in registers.
4. There are also very smooth transitions from one register to another, typically on a lick or on an improvised section.

Licks and Improvisation

1. There are long, improvisational melody lines that cover a wide vocal range and are filled with cascading runs and licks from both the blues and pentatonic scales. (See "pop coloratura" in Chapter 14, *Rock*, page 91.)
2. At the end of a phrase, there will either be an added note going up a step or down a third, or an intricate lick derived from the blues and/or pentatonic scales.

Vibrato

1. Diaphragmatic vibrato on the breath is typical on sustained tones, especially at the end of a phrase.
2. Delayed vibrato is characteristic.
3. A slower vibrato in a ballad is typical.
4. Shimmering vibrato is typical in faster tempo songs.
5. Vocal fold flutter vibrato is rarely used, but does exist in R&B, usually on faster passages.

Pronunciation

Conversational, colloquial, southern United States pronunciation is typical in rhythm & blues style.

R&B Artists

Dinah Washington, Aretha Franklin, Ray Charles, Patti Labelle, Jennifer Holiday, Michael Jackson, Barry White, Otis Redding, James Brown, Smokey Robinson, Al Green, The O'Jays, Marvin Gaye, Stevie Wonder, Gladys Knight and the Pips, Rufus and Chaka Khan, Teddy Pendergrass, Isaac Hayes, Earth, Wind and Fire, Ray Charles, Al Jarreau, B.B. King, Etta James, Tina Turner, Lou Rawls, The Temptations, The Penguins and Bill Withers.

Mary J. Blige, Brandy, R. Kelly, Sisqo, Toni Braxton, Lauryn Hill, Peabo Bryson, Babyface, TLC, Luther Vandross, Regina Belle, Anita Baker, Janet Jackson, Boyz II Men, Chaka Khan, Prince, James Ingram, N'Sync, Marc Anthony, En Vogue, Destiny's Child, Tracie Spencer, Brian McKnight, Whitney Houston, Aaliyah, Yolanda Adams, Keesha, Erykah Badu, Tamia, D'Angelo, Jill Scott, Monica, Mya, Sade, Alicia Keyes, Musiq, Soulchild, Usher, India, Beyonce, Cristina Aguilera, Arie and Mariah Carey.

CHAPTER TWENTY-ONE

Jazz

"The Vocal Power Singing Method opened my horizons and en-riched more so my personal singing and teaching. The method is simple and straight-to-the-point."

Anna Gotti
Professional singer & Singing teacher, Italy.
Vice President & International Coordinator of A.I.C.I.
Vocal Power Director, Europe

Jazz is an improvisational art, with its foundation rooted in the blues. In jazz, the voice is used like an instrument and the instruments are used like voices. They can laugh, cry, and moan. You need a very reliable and flexible vocal technique and a well trained ear to sing Jazz.

Vibrato

In jazz, singers use a variety of vibrato styles: Diaphragmatic throat, flutter, shimmering, or a combination of all four, even within the same song! The vibrato is also an "instrumental" way of using the voice in jazz: Slow, fast, wide and slow and wide and fast, straight tone and delayed vibrato.

A straight tone into a slow vibrato usually expresses loneliness. For example, you can use a straight tone into vibrato on the word, "Blue" to express loneliness in the song, "When Sunny Gets Blue" (by Fisher and Segal). A straight tone into slow vibrato speeding up into a fast vibrato usually expresses building excitement and is very effective at the end of a heart wrenching song. The shimmering vibrato is typical in faster songs and in *scatting* a tune.

Vocal Colors, Registers and Dynamics

If we think of the voice as an instrument, then of course all the vocal colors we possess should be used to express emotion in the words. A rainbow of vocal colors is used to express the meaning of the words in jazz. Head and chest registers, as well as the belt mix, are used in jazz. The jazz singer must also be versatile in the areas of vocal dynamics: Pianissimo (very soft) to fortissimo (very loud), crescendo (gradually soft to loud) and decrescendo (gradually loud to soft).

Your Personal Touch

In jazz, the composer writes a straight forward melody line and it is up to the singer to add creative elements. *Syncopation*, *anticipation* and *back-phrasing* can be used to put your own personal mark on a song. The audience is kept interested in your unique rendition and it may change at every performance!

Syncopation

Once a rhythm is established, deliberate accents on the weak beats (up beats) are re-ferred to as *syncopations*.

In the following example, there are 4 beats to a measure. The numbers are the *strong beats*, the *and's* are the *upbeats*: <u>**1**</u>- <u>***and***</u> - 2 - <u>***and***</u> - 3 - <u>***and***</u> - 4 - <u>***and***</u>. When the *and* is ac-cented, this creates a *syncopation*.

Musical example

A singer can create more interest in a song by using syncopations not written into the music, especially on the repeat of the tune. In Jazz you not only have the freedom to do this, but you are expected to be rhythmically creative. Remember, you are an instrument!

The composer often writes syncopations into the song. An example of this is in the song, "Don't Get Around Much Anymore," by Duke Ellington and Bob Russell. On the first measure, "Missed the Saturday dance," the downbeat is played by the accompaniment. The singer comes in on the *and* of 1. This "late" entrance also describes the person in the song having "Missed the Saturday Dance" and also missed the down beat. The music describes the action in the story.

Phrasing

On the sheet music, a song is usually simply laid out. It is up to the artist to make the lyric their own personal statement. You can think of it as pulling a phrase together, to shorten the time in which a phrase is sung and stretching out a phrase to lengthen the time in which a phrase is sung. It is important that you are aware of the chord changes under your melody line, so that you don't stretch or pull the phrase over chords that don't harmonize with notes in the phrase. Listen to the jazz greats to hear how this works. You can make a song more interesting by using creative phrasings, such as anticipation and back-phrasing.

Anticipation

Anticipation: Coming in before the downbeat in a measure. A singer can take a simple phrase and create more interest by using *anticipation*. It takes the *squareness* out of the song.

Back-Phrasing

Back-phrasing: Coming in after the down beat in a measure.

Improvising

You can improvise over the chords of a melody, once the original melody is established. The same words are used, but you can change the notes. It is important that you still sing a recognizable variation of the original melody. You can vary the words in improvisation as well.

Scatting

Scatting is vocal improvisation on a tune using nonsensical word syllables. In scatting, a singer can use his or her voice in an instrumental style by imitating the timbre (tone color) of instruments such as the trumpet, saxophone, trombone and guitar.

Scatting on a melody is done after you establish the original tune. It is on the repeat of a section of music, so that the listener is already familiar with the original melody. You must be very familiar with the chord progressions of the melody line in order to scat, weaving up and down and around the original melody line. Ella Fitzgerald is a singer known for her amazing scatting. She uses a variety of colors, registers, and vibrato. You can hear *shimmering* vibrato in her scat sections. You can hear her fine scatting in tunes such as "Lady be Good," by George and Ira Gershwin.

Another example of fine scatting is Grammy winning Jazz singer, Nenna Freelon. In a tune called, "Dad's Delight/Lil' B's poem," by E. Gibson, B. Hucherson and D. Carn, Nnenna truly uses her voice instrumentally. I would consider this example progressive jazz and not traditional jazz style.

Alliteration

Another stylistic feature of jazz singing style is *alliteration*, which is repetition of an initial sound in two or more words of a phrase. Sounds can be in the middle of words as well, as long as the sounds are within the same phrase. If you are aware of *alliteration,* you can bring more meaning to the words by using the sound of the words themselves.

A good example of *alliteration,* is in the song, "As Time Goes By, " by Herman Hupfeld.

In the phrase, "The world will always welcome lovers," there are four initial "w's." If you begin the "w" with an "oo," you will be more expressive by singing, "The oorld ooil alooays ooelcome lovers."

Consonants for Expression

A good jazz singer will give more emphasis to consonants for expression. You can sustain an "l," "m," and "n" with or without vibrato for a more sensual way of expressing the words. For example, there are five "l" sounds in this phrase: "The worlld will allways wellcome llovers.," also from the song, "As Time Goes By." By sustaining the "l" with vibrato you can make a more personal statement. Be careful that you don't over do and exaggerate every single "l."

The following words are regularly found in songs and by being aware of the underlined consonants, you will add more expression to the word.

Lovely, Love, Just, Sweet, Man, Never, Kiss, Baby, Please, Squeeze, Give, Got, Heart, Touch, Darling, Very, Rain and Feel, Make, Quiet, Stop, Crazy, Some and One.

Assonance is a partial rhyme where the stressed vowels are the same, but the consonants are different. For example, from the song, "Can't Help Lovin' That Man of Mine," by P. G. Wodehouse and Oscar Hammerstein II, "Maybe I'm crazy, maybe I know." You can use these same vowel sounds to color your words.

Inner rhymes are also a tool of expression. For example, from the song, "The Man I Love," by George Gershwin," Maybe Tuesday will be my good news day."

Onomatopoeia

Onomatopoeia, (pronounced "on a mot a peeya") is a word that sounds like the action. A good lyricist uses onomatopoeia to express the images in a song. For example, in "Choo, Choo Ch' Boogie," by Vaughn Horten, Denver Darling and Milton Gabler, you can imitate the sound of a train with the "Ch" sound.

In the song, "When Sunny gets Blue," by Fisher and Segal, the words, "pitter, patter" can sound like rain: "Pitter, patter, pitter, patter, love is gone, so what can matter?" You can create the sound of the rain by emphasizing the "p" and "t." Jazz composers are usually very good at *word painting,* since they recognize the voice to be an instrument, capable of expressing images and sounds.

Note: A jazz singer is expected to be a musician as well as a singer. You need to know the keys of your songs. You need to know how to give directions to your pianist or band. You should have a basic knowledge of music theory and ear training.

SING!

Guidelines for Working on a Jazz Song

1. Improvising - Establish the melody before improvising on it.
2. Back-phrasing - Be aware of the underlying chord progression as you pull and stretch your phrases over the chord.
3. Vibrato - You can use any or all of the following: diaphragmatic, throat, shimmering and flutter. The vibrato can be slow, fast, wide and slow, wide and fast. You can use straight tones and delayed vibrato.
4. Vocal colors - Use your four colors: chest, mouth, nasal and head to express the words.
5. Vocal dynamics - Your natural speech pattern will tell you what words to emphasize.
6. Alliteration - Be aware of vowels and consonants that sound alike within a phrase.
7. Onomatopoeia - Be aware of words that sound like the image and use them.
8. Scatting - Know your chord progressions. Study the scatting of established Jazz singers. Study improvisational techniques used by established instrumentalists as well as singers.
9. Syncopations - Learn the rhythms as written before you attempt to syncopate.
10. Use the "creaky door," "throat cry," "throat laugh," and "back l."

Jazz Artists

Ella Fitzgerald, Keely Smith, Louie Prima, Sarah Vaughn, Lena Horne, Peggy Lee, Rosemary Clooney, Billie Holiday, Mel Torme', Cleo Laine, Betty Carter, Sheila Jordan, Mark Murphy, Jon Hendricks, Jay Clayton, Alice Babs, Ivie Anderson, Jackie Cain, June Christy, Andy Bey, Blossom Dearie, Eddie Jefferson, Etta James, King Pleasure, Irene Kral, Lambert, Hendrick and Ross, Abbey Lincoln, Anita O'Day, Flora Purim, Betty Roche, Dennis Rowland, Jimmy Scott, Nancy Wilson, Nina Simone, Bessie Smith, Jo Stafford, Dinah Washington, Nat King Cole, Sammy Davis Jr., Frankie Laine, Billy Eckstein, Vic Damone, June Christy, Susanne McCorkle, Helen Merrill, Daryl Sherman, Michael Buble', Polly Bergen, Margaret Whiting, Rod Stewart, Pat Suzuki, Joe Williams, Tony Bennett, Carmen McRae, Louis Armstrong, Diane Schuur, Dee Dee Bridgewater, The Manhattan Transfer, Ann Hampton Calloway, Ruth Brown, Harry Connick Jr., Nneenna Freelon, Diane Reeves, Take 6, Natalie Cole, Cassandra Wilson, Al Jarreau, George Benson, Shirly Horn, Diana Krall, Kurt Elling, Bobby McFerrin, Madeline Eastman, Dominique Eade, Rachelle Ferrell, Carmen Lundy, Susannah McCorkle, Kevin Mahogany, Kitty Margolis, Dwight Trible, Judy Niemack, Rebecca Paris, Nancy King, Rhiannon, Jay Clayton, John Pizzarelli, Sheila Jordan, Peter Cincotti, Jamie Cullum, Curtis Stigers, Georgie Fame, Pinky Winters, Carol Sloane, Cathy Segal-Garcia, Ellen Johnson, Sue Rainey, Tierney Sutton.

CHAPTER TWENTY-TWO

Vibrato In Song

"Elisabeth Howard is simply one of the finest voice teachers in the world... her method and her track record have been and continue to be amazing."

John DeMain
Conductor, Madison Symphony, Madison Opera
Artistic Director, Opera Pacific; Conductor for Placido Domingo

(Singing Style CD, Track 40)

Vibrato is an element of style and is used as a tool of expression. The speed and width of vibrato may vary within any given song, depending upon the emotional intensity and musical style. From commercial/pop to classical style, a faster vibrato is used for more excitement and a slower vibrato is used for less energetic expressions. Singers have many choices. Vibrato shouldn't be an accident, just as the use of vocal color and dynamics are not accidents. They are choices, and come from emotional expression.

There is a great advantage to having good vibrato control when considering musical style. For example:

1. In traditional music theater, vibrato is usually diaphragmatic on sustained tones. Throat vibrato is heard as well on shorter notes. A shimmering vibrato is used for more intensity.

2. In classical singing, diaphragmatic vibrato is typical on long, sustained tones and a shimmering vibrato is used on fast passing notes. Throat vibrato is not typical.

3. A vocal fold flutter vibrato is almost never used in music theater or in classical singing. It can be heard in some pop singers' styles.

4. The straight tone with no vibrato is often used by a comic character in a musical or an opera. Rock singers typically use straight tones with very little vibrato.

5. The delayed vibrato is more typical of pop style.

In classical singing, a slow and wide vibrato is used only for comic character roles, usually depicting an older person. In commercial/pop music, an example of a slow and wide vibrato is the singing of the pop group, the Bee Gees. The tempo and lyric of the song usually suggests to the singer the type of vibrato most appropriate: fast, slow, wide, narrow, etc. In all styles of vocal music, a vibrato that gradually *speeds* up, adds intensity to the moment. This technique is heard typically in opera at the end of an exciting aria. Sometimes the pitch is even purposely *sharped* (raised) ever so slightly to heighten the intensity.

To increase your vibrato control, work with Chapter 6 (page 43) and the accompanying *Singing Techniques CD.*

Vibrato in the Recording Studio

The ability to control vibrato is crucial in the recording studio. A professional session singer may be asked to sing with a straight tone, a delayed vibrato, a vibrato that speeds up, a faster vibrato, a slower vibrato, a sustained tone with vibrato with a crescendo or a decrescendo or a vibrato with sudden dynamic changes, or to synchronize the vibrato speed with the lead singer or with other singers in a group.

Vibrato Styles Review

1. *Vocal fold flutter* is found in the American folk songs of the 70's, French cabaret chansons (songs), Spanish flamenco, and some Mid-Eastern singing.
2. *Throat vibrato* is found in jazz standards, classical (minimal) and pop.
3. *Shimmering vibrato* is typical in faster songs in all styles including classical style and is typical in jazz scatting.
4. *Diaphragmatic vibrato* on the breath is found in almost all vocal styles from classical to rock.
5. *Diaphragmatic vibrato* on the breath is usually combined with some *throat* or *shimmering vibrato* for a faster speed and more intensity.

Notes:
1. We aren't born with vibrato.
2. Vibrato can be taught and learned like any other vocal skill.
3. Vibrato and straight tones are tools of expression.
4. There are at least four vocal techniques for vibrato which vary with musical style.

Sing and have fun!

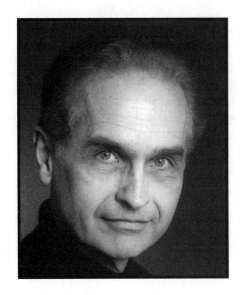

CHAPTER TWENTY-THREE

Classical Singing

"Elisabeth Howard's students learn quickly and sing artistically. Most importantly, their voices stay healthy year after year in any style of music. Although I have taught singing for decades, I'm still learning from my inspiring friend."

John Glenn Paton
Emeritus Professor of Voice, University of Colorado
Editor, Vocal Masterworks, Alfred Publishing
Lecturer, University of Southern California

(Singing Style CD, Tracks 41-44)

In classical singing, emphasis is placed on beauty of tone, vocal skill, musicianship, acting and passion. In a performance of classical vocal music, there is very little flexibility for improvisation. The composer has written notes, rhythms, tempos and dynamics, all of which must be adhered to closely by the performer. Notes and words are rarely changed to suit the singer. In opera, there are no key transpositions to accommodate the range of the singer. If the aria is written with a "high C," you must have a dependable "high C." The audience usually knows where that "high C" is in the opera and waits very anxiously to hear it. Even if the singer has a dependable high C, he or she may only hold the note longer than written when there is a *fermata* sign (see fermata on page 123) over the note, or by agreement with the conductor and must be well rehearsed.

A singer can take some liberties, provided the choices are in keeping with the traditional musical style of the period, and providing there is agreement with the accompanist or conductor so that there are no "surprises" at the performance. In opera, very often these liberties become part of the traditional performance of the aria (song) and set a precedent for all others to follow, particularly if the liberty involves vocal prowess, such as holding that "high C" longer for dramatic effect, and if you are well known.

Coloratura

The use of fast melodic passages, involving scales, arpeggios, trills and staccati are part of an operatic style called *coloratura*, which are outbursts of emotion expressed in florid, fast musical passages and show off the singers' virtuosity. Coloratura is typical of the bel canto style of early 19th century composers such as Giacomo Rossini, Vincenzo Bellini and Gaetano Donizetti. Traditionally, these flourishes are written by the composer, but the singer may also compose his or her own coloratura variations on a given melody. Even though these passages sound spontaneous, they are well rehearsed. Coloratura passages are rarely altered by the singer "on the spot" at a performance.

In the past, the word, "coloratura," has also meant a light, agile soprano, but in recent years, all classical singers, men and women alike, are expected to be able to sing coloratura passages.

Coloratura technique

The technique I use for teaching coloratura is similar to techniques used for the flutter vibrato. The vocal folds, instead of creating a rapid flutter vibrato on one note, flutter to articulate the notes in rapid scales and arpeggios. A slight, inaudible "h" is used to articulate each note in these passages.

The Da Capo Aria

Ornamentation and embellishments are typical in vocal music of the Baroque period (1550-1750) in the music of composers such as George Frederick Handel and Henry Purcell. These ornamentations and embellishments are typically performed on the repeat section of the music. For example, in the "da capo aria," the singer returns to the beginning of the piece, singing the melody and adding his or her own embellishments through to the end of the piece.

Note: According to Will Crutchfield, musicologist and conductor, in an article in *Opera News* states that the singers in that period embellished the melody from the beginning of the piece.

Choral Music

In fast passages in choral singing, as in the music of Johann Sebastian Bach and George Frederick Handel, coloratura is done with the technique similar to the diaphragmatic pulses of vibrato on each note. These faster passages are not categorized as "coloratura," because they are slower than the coloratura passages in bel canto arias. But you can see the importance of having a technique for singing these faster passages in order to be "in sync" as a group.

The Trill

(Singing Style CD, Track 42)

A trill is an ornamentation that is produced by alternating rapidly between 2 notes, either a whole step or a half step apart. It may appear as an incidental ornament of short duration, for example, the length of a quarter note, or it may sustain for several measures.

Sing: Whole Step Trill

It would appear in the music as:

Sing: Half Step Trill

It would appear in the music as:

On the staff, a trill sign is written above the note to indicate the trill. A sharp or a flat sign may appear as well, if the other note in the trill is a note that is not in the key. For example, in the key of A major, there are three sharps, but if the composer wants you to trill on E and F natural, he must indicate the F natural within the trill sign. Otherwise, the trill would be from E to F sharp.

Since a trill is rapidly alternating from one pitch to another, we need to hear both pitches. A trill sometimes gives the impression of having an accent or pulse on each beat in a measure.

You can also build intensity into a trill by starting slowly and then gradually speed up. A trill should not sound like a vibrato. If you play an instrument like the piano, play the trill on your instrument first, as this helps you to define the individual pitches when you sing.

How to Trill

I have found the best way of singing a trill accurately, is to anchor the tone on the lower pitch while listening for the upper pitch. The trill is a rapid throat vibrato. But the distance in pitch for the throat vibrato is no more than a quarter of a pitch wide, while the trill is the distance from one note to the other, either an interval of a half step or a whole step.

Trill Exercises

1. In the following exercise, start with quarter notes and speed up to sixteenth notes.

Sing:

2. Now repeat the above exercise. Begin with sixteenth notes and speed up to thirty-second notes (double the speed).

Staccato

(Singing Style CD, Track 43)

The staccato is a short detached note, written with a dot above or below it to indicate a reduction of its duration by half.

Musical Example:

Staccato technique

The staccato is done with the same abdominal pulses, in the solar plexus area, not the lower stomach, that we use for diaphragmatic vibrato. The support must be steady. Staccato is not done by the throat muscles and there is a sense of open vocal folds.

Staccato Exercises:

1. On the vowel "ah" (as in "far"),

Sing:

2. Repeat, beginning a half step higher each time.

Helpful Hints for Staccato

1. Use steady support and don't bounce the staccato notes.
2. An inaudible "h," will help you to avoid a glottal attack on each note.
3. For your highest notes, it helps to *think* air through your vocal folds and a yawn. Lift the soft palate. If the vocal folds are holding too firm on high notes, the tone will stop.
4. For your highest notes, the mouth position needs to be in a smile, eye teeth showing.
5. Use a slight "oh" [ɔ] just before your higher notes for a warmer tone.
6. The whole phrase must flow smoothly and the individual pitches must be accurate.

The Cadenza

(Singing Style CD, Track 44)

The *Cadenza* (Cadence) is an elaborate melodic embellishment, used at the end of an aria to add excitement and to show off the singer's vocal ability. It must be set and well rehearsed with the musical director. The cadenza involves fast melodic passages consisting of scales, arpeggios, trills and/or staccati.

Here is the ending of an aria, as written:

Sing:

With a cadenza added,

Sing:

The Turn

The turn is an ornament made up of 4 or 5 notes surrounding a principal note. It consists of the note above, the written note, and the note below, returning to the written note on the beat.

Sing:

The Appoggiatura

The appoggiatura is a grace note that does not belong to the chord, called a non-chord tone, and occurs on the downbeat. It is usually one note above or below the note written on the staff, resolving to the written note. There are two types–the long appoggiatura and the short appoggiatura or "grace note appoggiatura."

Sing: Long appoggiatura

Sing: Short appoggiatura

The Fermata

The *Fermata* (⌒) means that you can sustain the note longer than the written value on the sheet music. How long to hold the note is by mutual agreement between the singer and the accompanist or musical director. Holding a note longer is usually at a dramatic peak in the song or aria and gives the singer the opportunity, not only to display his or her vocal ability, but is an opportunity for emotional impact.

Guidelines for Singing Coloratura

1. Break down the passage of notes into smaller musical groupings. Often you can see a repeating pattern in the music. This is called a *sequence*. For example: C - D - E - F; D - E - F - G; E - F - G - A - F. This sequence uses notes from the C Major scale beginning on the first note. Each four note pattern begins on the next step of the C Major scale, finally reaching its goal and resolving to the F. The steps of the scale would be:
1 - 2 - 3 - 4; 2 - 3 - 4 - 5; 3 - 4 - 5 - 6 - 4. Work on each four note pattern first making sure the pitches are accurate and in tune.
2. On very fast legato or smooth vocal lines, the vocal folds "articulate" the individual notes. Use the flutter vibrato technique to articulate. If you try to sing these fast passages without articulating each note, you will experience sliding from note to note, causing inaccuracy in pitch.
3. The support remains steady, not bounced.
4. The throat is open and does not help with articulation of the notes.
5. The tongue must not press down in the back of the throat. Think toward "ee" [i] for the correct tongue position.

Note: Musicianship is of utmost importance in singing coloratura passages. You must be able to "hear" these scales and arpeggios in order to sing them. You can only sing what you can hear. Those singers who play an instrument have an advantage in being able to hear scales, intervals, chords and rhythm.

Classical Artists

Sopranos - Lyric and Dramatic

Eileen Farrell, Anna Moffo, Renée Fleming, Elizabeth Schwarzkopf, Renata Tebaldi, Mirella Freni, Angela Gheorghiu, Lisa Della Casa, Montserrat Caballe, Kiri te Kanawa, Birgit Nilsson, Victoria de los Angeles, Maria Callas, Eleanor Steber, Leonie Rysanek, Licia Alabanese, Deborah Voigt, Elizabeth Futral, Erie Mills, Carol Vaness, Renata Scotto, Patricia Racette, Dawn Upshaw, Kirsten Flagstad, Grace Bumbry, Kathleen Battle, Lucine Amara, Martina Arroyo, Barbara Bonney, Elly Ameling, Zinka Milanov.

Coloratura Sopranos

Beverly Sills, Roberta Peters, Natalie Dessay, Graziella Sciutti, Joan Sutherland, Sumi Jo, Rita Streich, Luisa Tetrazzini, Amelita Galli - Curci.

Mezzo sopranos and Contraltos

Cecelia Bartoli, Marilyn Horne, Denyce Graves, Susanne Mentzer, Susan Graham, Frederica von Stade, Lilli Chookasian, Mignon Dunn, Jennifer Larmore, Anne Sophie Von Otter, Vasselina Kasarova, Rosalind Elias, Christa Ludwig, Regina Resnik, Kathleen Ferrier, Janet Baker, Fiorenza Cossotto, Rise Stevens, Grace Bumbry, Teresa Berganza, Helen Traubel, Shirley Verrett.

Tenors

Roberto Alagna, Luciano Pavarotti, Fritz Wunderlich, Jose Carreras, Placido Domingo, Franco Corelli, Ben Heppner, Ramon Vargas, Cesare Valetti, Mario Del Monaco, Nikolai Gedda, Mario Lanza, Alfredo Kraus, Enrico Caruso, Paul Groves, Richard Tucker, Luigi Alva, Jan Peerce, George Shirley.

Baritones

Sherrill Milnes, Giuseppi de Luca, Dietrich Fischer – Dieskau, Robert Merrill, Tito Gobbi, Fernando Corena, George London, Cornell MacNeil, Thomas Quastoff, Thomas Allen, Thomas Hampson, Rod Gilfry.

Basses

Samuel Ramey, Nikolai Ghiaurov, Cesare Siepi, Leonard Warren, Paul Robeson.

ABC's of Vocal Harmony by Elisabeth Howard

For the building blocks of good musicianship work at home or in your car with "ABCs of Vocal Harmony," by Elisabeth Howard. This is a book accompanied by 4 CDs which is written especially for singers. This course is an excellent foundation in ear training and sight reading and will give you the tools you need to be a singer who is also a musician. It covers scales, intervals, chords and rhythms. Each CD is one hour long and has male and female vocal demonstrations, explanations, exercises and piano accompaniment.

"ABCs of Vocal Harmony," by Elisabeth Howard is also an excellent review for the more advanced student. Order at your nearest book or music store.

CHAPTER TWENTY-FOUR

Vocal Health Guidelines

*"The Vocal Power Method training clearly demonstrates the differ-
ing techniques in blues, pop, jazz and classical music. Elisabeth
Howard trains the voice in a healthy way."*

Hege Tunaal
Professional Ballad Singer; Faculty, Oslo National College of the Arts

1. If your voice is tired or hoarse, rest it totally, if possible. Do not talk or sing or even whisper. Whispering causes further hoarseness. Mark your music at rehearsals. That is, go through the music with a gentle but clear tone. Singing with a breathy tone will dry out the mucous membranes of the vocal folds. A wonderfully performed rehearsal is not worth a bad performance ... or no performance at all!

2. Herbs such as Echinacea and Zinc are effective in warding off a cold, since they support the immune system. Capsules are more concentrated than tea which is also good, since it is warm.

3. Warm beverages soothe the throat area. Not too hot. "Throat Coat" tea is excellent, especially during rehearsals and performances.

4. Gargling with warm salt water is good for a sore throat. You can also gargle with a menthol or eucalyptus based mouthwash. Many singers find throat sprays such as Entertainer's Secret to be excellent for dry throat or hoarseness.

5. You can use a vaporizer or the old - fashioned way - a towel over your head, inhaling the vapors from hot water containing menthol or eucalyptus. An ointment such as Ben-Gay, spread on the throat and chest with a towel over the area is very effective in treating a sore throat or cough, especially if you stay warm and perspire, allowing the vapors to relieve cold symptoms.

6. When singing with amplified accompaniment such as a band, be sure to have a good monitoring system. A small speaker or two, facing toward you as you sing, allows you to hear yourself. Without this system, you may get the impression that you can't be heard above the other amplified instruments and there will be a tendency to push air for volume, which will adversely affect your voice.

7. Try to *feel* how you sing so that you memorize the sensations of healthy singing. Don't sing for hours and hours. If you have to rehearse that long, just mark it.

8. Ideally, a singer should have eight or nine hours of sleep. Sometimes it is impossible, especially if you are traveling, but that is what I recommend for keeping your voice rested. Your voice depends on the health of your body and mind.

9. Smoking cuts the breath power and dries out the vocal folds. Need I say more? Don't do it!

Stay healthy, keep singing and HAVE FUN!

LET IT SHINE!

SING!

NOTES

CHAPTER TWENTY-FIVE

Vocal Glossary

"The Vocal Power Method has helped me immensely. In particular, it has smoothed out my vibrato, made it possible for me to sing with resonance, good breath and dynamics control, and different vocal colorings. Most importantly, the method has allowed me to enjoy singing more than ever."

Chauncey Isom
Singer/Songwriter, Los Angeles, California

Abduct: To move the vocal folds apart.

Adduct: To bring the vocal folds together.

Alliteration: Repetition of a consonant in two or more words of a phrase. Medial consonants also create alliteration. The consonants may be initial, medial or final.

Alto: Lower female voice in a four-part chorus.

Anticipation: Coming in before the downbeat.

Approximate: To bring the vocal folds close together. Same as adduct.

Articulation: Physically forming speech sounds.

Back L: Vocal quality produced by back tongue downward pressure for non-classical singing.

Back-phrasing: Coming in after the downbeat.

Baritone: Male voice lower than a tenor and higher than a bass.

Bass: (1) Lower male voice in a four-part chorus, (2) Lowest note of a chord, (3) Lowest part of a musical texture, (4) An instrument that plays that part, e.g., string bass or bass guitar.

Basso profundo: Deep bass, sings strongly below the bass staff.

Bel canto: Beautiful singing, especially in the classical style.

Belt mix: Combination of head and chest registers for loud, high, energized singing to match the chest register.

Bernoulli effect: Suction produced by the fact that air moving through a narrow passage has less pressure than air that is not in motion.

Break: Abrupt change in vocal quality when moving from one register to the other.

Breastbone (sternum): Bone to which the ribs join in front.

Breath management: Efficient use of air.

Chest color: Vibrations in the chest, resonating in the vocal tract.

"Chest lean": Concept of "leaning" air against breastbone, giving more depth to tone.

Chest mix: A "belt mix" with more vocal fold firmness than "head mix," therefore closer to chest register.

Chest register: Lower tones characterized by shortened, thickened vocal folds. So-called because sympathetic vibrations can be felt in the chest/thorax when this register is used.

Chest voice: Lower register, *modal voice, alto, voce di petto* (It.), *voix de poitrine* (Fr.)

Color (timbre): Variable aspect of vocal quality, ranging from bright to dark, produced by subtle factors of vowel formation and tone production in response to tonal imagination, and contributing to emotional communication.

Coloratura: Singing very fast scales, arpeggios, trills, etc.

Coloratura soprano: The highest soprano type. Sings above high C, above the treble staff.

Contralto: Lowest female voice. Lower and deeper than a mezzo-soprano.

Countertenor: A male voice that sings primarily in the same range as a female alto.

"Creaky Door": Bringing the vocal folds together just enough to create the sound of a creaky door.

Dialect: Pronunciation typical of a specific locality or social class.

Diaphragm: Large dome-shaped muscle that provides a floor for the thorax (chest). Partition between the thorax and the abdomen.

Diaphragmatic breathing: Breathing by descent of the diaphragm and contraction of the abdominal muscles in alternation. .

Diaphragmatic vibrato on the breath: Slight solar plexus pulses inducing a wave-like sound through the vocal folds.

Diphthong: Vowel sounds pronounced one after the other within one syllable, therefore on one note.

Dynamics: Volume levels, loud to soft.

Falsetto: Lightest register of the male voice. Authorities use this term in various ways.

Floating ribs: Two lowest ribs (11th and 12th) attached to the spine at the back, but not to any other bone.

Focus: "Edge," "core," "ring," in the tone.

Focusing: Adducting or approximating the vocal folds for clarity of tone.

Forward placement: Mask resonance, *maschera* (It.); having nasal/mouth resonance. Singing with both the nasal and mouth resonance and with sensations of vibration in the face.

Genre: Specific style.

Glottal attack: Closed vocal folds suddenly "pop open" resulting in obvious onset.

Glottis: Space between the vocal folds.

Hard palate: The bony, forward part of the roof of the mouth.

Head color: Vibrations in the head, resonating in the vocal tract.

Head mix: A "belt mix" with less vocal fold firmness than "chest mix," therefore closer to head register.

Head register: Portion of the vocal range characterized by thinly stretched vocal folds. So-called because of a sensation of vibrations in the head.

Head voice: (It.) voce di testa, (Fr.) voix de tete, upper register , soprano voice, falsetto,.

Hyoid bone: U-shaped bone to which the root of the tongue is attached and from which the thyroid cartilage is suspended.

Improvisation: Making up melodies, usually based on original melody.

Intercostals: Three sets of muscles between the ribs. Externi are inspiratory. Interni and intimi are expiratory.

Larynx (voice box): Structure of cartilage and muscles, containing the vocal folds; visible externally as the Adam's Apple.

"Lick": Melodic embellishment on a syllable or a word in non-classical improvisation.

Lip vowel: Vowel sound shaped by rounding the lips to some degree.

Lower mix: The sound the lower register can produce to match the head voice quality.

Lower register: See chest voice.

Lyric soprano: The most frequently found high female voice. So-called by association with melodic (lyric) singing.

Lyric tenor: The most frequently found high male voice.

Mezzo-soprano: Female voice that is slightly lower and heavier than a soprano voice.

Mixed register: Combination of head and chest register.

Mouth color: Vibrations in the mouth, resonating in the vocal tract.

Nasal color: Vibrations in the nose, resonating in the vocal tract.

Onset: Beginning of a tone.

Open throat: Large pharynx, producing a desirable sensation of unimpeded singing.

Onomatopoeia: Words imitating natural sounds.

Passaggio (passageway, It.): Transition between head and chest registers.

Pharynx (throat): Resonator above the larynx and behind the mouth, consisting of laryngo-pharynx, oro-pharynx, and naso-pharynx. (Vennard).

Phrasing: Grouping of words and melodic tones.

Placement: Mentally directing the tone to a particular resonance or vibrating area.

Placement track: Vibrations felt from the lowest to the highest notes of the voice through chest, mouth, nasal and head vibrations.

"Pop coloratura": Technique for singing rapid coloratura passages in non-classical music.

Preparation: A state of readiness to sing, the moment before the sound is produced.

Register: See head register and chest register.

Resonance: Reinforcement and prolongation of a sound by reflection or by vibration of other bodies. (Webster's dictionary) The intensification and enriching of a musical tone.

Resonant: Vibrant, sonorous.

Rib breathing: Breathing by moving the ribs. Costal breathing.

Root of the tongue: Back part of the tongue, including the lower part of the tongue that is out of sight.

Scatting: Improvising on a tune, using syllables rather than words.

Shimmering vibrato: A fast throat vibrato.

Silent H: Voiceless consonant. In this book used for onset at beginning of phrase on a word beginning with a vowel.

Soft palate: Soft part of the roof of the mouth, just behind the hard palate.

Solar plexus: Nerve complex at the pit of the stomach.

Soprano: Higher female voice in a four-part chorus.

Subglottic: Below the glottis.

Support: A dynamic balance between muscles of inhalation and exhalation.

Tenor: Higher male voice in a four-part chorus.

"Throat cry": Feeling of a "cry" in the pharynx, used for expression

"Throat laugh": Feeling of a "laugh" in the pharynx, used for expression.

Throat vibrato: Pulsating pharyngeal walls involved in wave-like tone.

Thyroid cartilage: Largest cartilage of the larynx, seen and felt as the Adam's Apple.

Tongue: Organ occupying the floor of the mouth, and attached to the jaw, hyoid bone, pharynx, and soft palate. It is composed of many muscles and can assume many shapes, useful for mastication (chewing) and articulation.

Tongue vowel: Vowel sound articulated by raising the tongue to some degree.

Upper mix: Combination of head and chest register on high notes to match chest register.

Upper register: See head voice.

Uvula: Bit of muscle hanging from the velum.

Vibrato: Wave-like pulse in a sustained tone.

Vocal fold flutter vibrato: Rapid interruptions in the adduction of the vocal folds.

Vocal folds (cords, bands, lips): Valve-like organs in the larynx, which can close the top of the windpipe or can vibrate to produce phonation.

Vocal tract: Series of interconnected resonating cavities from the glottis to the lips.

Voiceprint: Visual representation of vocal tone, as measured by a spectrograph, said to be as individual as a fingerprint.

Voiced consonant: Consonant that employs vocal fold vibration.

Voiceless consonant: Consonant that does not require the vocal folds to vibrate.

SING!

NOTES

CHAPTER TWENTY-SIX

Musical Glossary

"In a very short amount of time, Elisabeth Howard has given me the voice, wide octave range and vibrato I never knew I had. With her extraordinarily effective and unique techniques, her precise guidance and commitment to bringing out the best in her students, she has helped me achieve a life-long dream. I can now, proudly and honestly, call myself a singer."

Cheryl Christiansen
Singer/Song Writer; songs recorded by Diana Ross, Gladys Knight, Johnny Mathis and for feature films

A cappella: Without accompaniment.

Accel. (accelerando): Becoming gradually faster.

Adagio: A slow tempo, faster than largo and slower than andante.

Ad lib. (ad libitum): Freedom to vary from strict tempo.
Agitato: Agitated.

Al coda: To the coda.

Al fine: To the end.

Allargando: Growing gradually slower.

Allegro: Lively, quick or fast tempo.

Al segno: Go to the sign.

Andante: Moderately slow.
Animato: Animated.

Arp. (arpeggio): The notes of a chord played one at a time in succession.

Aria: A solo vocal piece in classical style usually associated with an opera or oratorio.

A tempo: Return to original or normal tempo after a ritard or ad lib. section.

Break: Instrumental interlude within a song.

Cadence: The final two or three chords ending a composition.

Cadenza: An extended vocal section in free, improvisatory style, usually at the end of a classical aria.

Chart: Usually refers to sheet music containing only the chord progressions of a song, written above the measures. The chart may or may not include melody line and lyrics.

Coda: An added section of music concluding the piece.

Colla voce: (Italian for "with the voice") accompaniment is to follow singer's tempo.

Cresc. (crescendo): Growing gradually louder.

Cue: Musical, verbal or visual communication between singer and musicians.

D.C. (da capo): (Play again) from the beginning of the music.

SING!

Decresc. (decrescendo): Gradually decreasing volume.

Dim. (diminuendo): Same as decrescendo.

D.S. (dal segno): Sing the section of music preceded by the sign,

Fermata (͡): Sustain longer than written note..

"Fill": Improvised melody played by an accompanying instrument in between the sung phrases.

Fine: End of piece.

Forte (f): Loud.

Fortissimo (ff): Very loud.

Gliss. (glissando): Sliding from one pitch to another.

Hook: Memorable, catchy musical and/or verbal phrase, mostly used in non-classical music.

Intro. (introduction): Opening accompaniment leading to the entrance of the singer.

Largo: Very slow tempo.

Legato: Sing or play smoothly and connected.

Lento, Lent: Slow tempo.

Meno: Less.

Mezza voce: Sing at moderate volume.

Mezzo forte (mf): Moderately loud.

Mezzo piano (mp): Moderately soft.

Molto: Very (e.g. molto allegro - very fast tempo).

Non troppo: Not too much (e.g. non troppo allegro - not too fast).

Piano (p): Soft.
Pianissimo (pp): Very soft.
Piu: More (e.g., piu forte - louder).

Poco: Little (e.g., poco allegro - a little faster).

Poco a poco: Little by little (e.g., poco a poco forte - gradually louder).

Presto: Very fast tempo.

Railroad Tracks (//): Abrupt, completely silent pause in the music, a cesura.

Rall. (rallentando): Gradually slowing down.

Repeat sign (||): Indicates one repetition of the musical section between the :
at the beginning of the section and :   at the end of the section.

"Riff": A repeating melodic or rhythmic figure used in non-classical music.

Rit. (Ritard, Ritardando): Same as rallentando.

Rubato: Flexibility and freedom of tempo, similar to ad lib.

Sforzando (sf, sfz): Strong accent on a single note or chord.

Sost. (sostenuto): Momentarily sustaining and slackening the tempo.

Staccato: Detached and short note, indicated by a dot above or below the note, a reduction of its written duration by half.

Subito: Sudden, immediate (e.g., subito piano suddenly soft).

Syncopation: Accents on the weak beats

Tacet: Silence.

Tag: A short added ending to a piece, used in non-classical music.

Ten. (tenuto): Hold, sustain.

Tessitura: The general range in which the majority of notes lie in a song, aria, etc.

Vamp: Repeating musical pattern, used as an intro to a song, between verses or as entrance and exit music, used in non-classical music.

Vivace: Fast and lively tempo.

SING!

NOTES

CHAPTER TWENTY-SEVEN

Practice Phrases

"Vocal Power really condenses and simplifies singing for me. It's no wonder why so many of her students have success with their vocal careers and goals."

Vy Doan
International Vietnamese Singer/Performer

Practice phrases

...Day by day by ... day by day by ..

...Why oh why oh ... why oh why oh ...

..Now and then and ... now and then and ...

...On and on and ... on and on and ...

...There and then and ... there and then and ...

...His and hers and ... his and hers and ...

...You and me and ... you and me and ...

...Stores and floors and ... stores and floors and ...

...Stars and stripes and. ... stars and stripes and ...

For Kids

....Dog and cat and...Dog and cat and...

...Cat and mouse and...Cat and mouse and...

...Mouse and cheese and...mouse and cheese and...

...Mom and Dad and...Mom and Dad and...

...Boy and girl and...Boy and girl and...

...Sleep and play and...sleep and play and...

...Run and jump and...run and jump and...

...Spell and read and...spell and read and...

...Read and learn and...Read and learn and...

SING!

NOTES

Selected Bibliography

Alchin, Carolyn A., revised by Jones, Vincent. **Applied Harmony**. Los Angeles: L.R. Jones, 1935.

Apel, Willi. **Harvard Dictionary of Music**. Cambridge, Massachusettes: Harvard University Press, 1961.

Appelman, D. Ralph. **The Science of Vocal Pedagogy**. Bloomington: Indiana University Press, 1967.

Ayola, Edward L.. **Winning Rhythms**. San Diego, CA: KJOS West, 1985.

Burns, Ken. Jazz, A Film. USA: Florentine Films, 2000.

Carr, Roy. A Century of Jazz. New York: Da Capo Press, 1997.

Caruso, Enrico and Tetrazzini, Luisa. **Caruso and Tetrazzini on the Art of Singing**. New York: Dover Publications, Inc., 1975.

Charters, Samuel B.. **The Country Blues**. New York: Da Capo Press, 1975.

Cheng, Stephen. **The Tao of Voice**. Rochester, Vermont: Destiny Books, 1991.

Cole, Samuel W. and Lewis, Leo R.. **Melodia**. USA: Oliver Ditson Company, 1909.

Driggs, Frank and Lewine, Harris. **Black Beauty, White Heat**. New York: Da Capo Press, 1982.

Forward, Geoffrey G.. **American Diction for Singers**. Los Angeles: Alfred Publishing Company, Inc., 2001.

Forward, Geoffrey G.. **Power Speech**. Los Angeles: Performing Arts Global Publishing, 1987

Geralnick, Peter. **Last Train to Memphis**. New York: Little Brown and Company, 1994.

Gerou, Tom and Lusk, Linda. **Essential Dictionary of Music Notation**. Los Angeles: Alfred Publishing Company, Inc., 1996.

Giddins, Gary. **Riding on a Blue Note**. New York: Oxford University Press, 1981.

Giddens, Gary. **Visions of Jazz**. New York: Oxford University Press, 1998

Grout, Donald and Palisca, Claude V.. **A History of Western Music**. Mew York: W.W. Norton & Company, 1988

Hagen, Uta. **Respect for Acting**. New York: Macmillan Publishing Co., Inc., 1973.

Harmen, Alec, with Anthony Milner, and Mellers, Wilfrid. **Man and His Music**. New York: Oxford University Press, 1962.

Harnsberger, Lindsey C.. **Essential Dictionary of Music**. Los Angeles: Alfred Publishing Company, Inc., 1966.

Hindemith, Paul. **Elementary Training for Musicians**. New York: Belwin-Mills Publishing Corp., 1949.

Jadassohn. **A Manual of Harmony**. New York: G. Schirmer, 1893.

Jones, Daniel. **The Pronunciation of English**. Cambridge: Cambridge University Press, 1980.

Kenyon, John Samuel and Knott, Thomas Albert. **A Pronouncing Dictionary of American English**. Springfield: G. & C. Merriam Company, Publishers, 1953.

Lamperti, Giovanni Battista. **Vocal Wisdom Maxims of Giovanni Battista Lamperti.** Transcribed by William Earl Brown. Edited by Lillian Strongin. New York: Taplinger Publishing Company, 1957.

Lehmann, Lilli. **How to Sing**. New York: The Macmillan Company, 1955.

Lessac, Arthur. **The Use and Training of the Human Voice**. New York: DBS Publications, Inc., 1967.

Linklater, Kristin. **Freeing the Natural Voice**. New York: Drama Book Specialists (Publishers), 1976.

Marafioti, P. Mario. **Caruso's Method of Voice Production**. New York: Dover Publications, Inc., 1949.

Marshall, Madeleine. **The Singer's Manual of English Diction**. New York: Schirmer Books, 1953.

Mehegan, John. **Jazz Rhythm and the Improvised Line**. New York: Watson-Guptill Publications, 1962.

Meisner, Sanford and Longwell, Dennis. **Sanford Meisner on Acting**. New York: Vintage Books, 1987.

Miller, Richard. **The Structure of Singing.** New York: Schirmer Books, 1996

NBC Handbook of Pronunciation. Revised and updated by Eugene Ehrlich and Raymond Hand, Jr.. New York: Harper & Row, Publishers, 1984.

New Grove Dictionary of Opera, The. Sadie, Stanley, editor. New York: Groves Dictionaries of Music Inc., 1992.

Ottman, Robert W.. **Music for Sight Singing**. Englewood Cliffs, NJ: Prentice-Hall, Inc., 1956.

Palmer, Robert. **Deep Blues**. New York: Penguin Books, 1981.

Paton, John Glenn . **Foundations in Singing**. New York: MGraw-Hill, 2001.

Piston, Walter. Christy, Van A.. **Foundations in Singing**. Revised by John Glenn Paton. Dubuque: Wm. C. Brown Publishers. 1990. **Harmony**. New York: W.W. Norton & Company, 1962.

Stanislavski, Constantin. **An Actor Prepares**. Translated by Elizabeth Reynolds Hapgood. New York: Theatre Arts Books, 1948.

Stanislavski, Constantin. **Building a Character**. Translated by Elizabeth Reynolds Hapgood. New York: Theatre Arts Books, 1949.

Shemel, Sidney and Drasilovsky, M. William. **The Business of Music**. New York: Billboard Publications, Inc., 1971.

Stanislavski, Constantin. **Creating a Role**. Translated by Elizabeth Reynolds Hapgood. New York: Theatre Arts Books, 1961.

Sundberg, Johan. **The Science of the Singing Voice**. Dekalb, Illinois: Northern Illinois University Press, 1987.

Vennard, William. **Singing, the Mechanism and the Technic**. Boston: Carl Fischer, Inc., 1967.

Wardlow, Gayle Dean. **Chasin' That Devil Music**. San Francisco, CA: Miller Freeman Books, 1998.

Whitcomb, Ian. **After the Ball**. New York: Limelight Editions, 1972.

Wilson, Pat. **The Singing Voice**. London: Nick Hern Books Ltd., 1997.

Index

"To understand the power of the mix, is to understand the power of the voice!"

Tanner Redman
Actor/singer St. Louis MUNY; Pepperdine University student

(Continued from back cover)

taught at **Indiana University** and **Hunter College, NYC** and was a guest faculty member at University of Southern California in Los Angeles. She is past President of the Los Angeles Chapter of the **National Association of Teachers of Singing (NATS)**, is a voting member of **The National Academy of Recording Arts and Sciences (NARAS)**, a member of **Actors' Equity Association (AEA)** and **The American Federation of Television and Radio Artists (AFTRA)**.

Ms. Howard laid out the foundations of her Vocal Power Method of Singing in 1980 with the original publishing of the book SING!, which has enjoyed universal critical acclaim. Over the past 25 years she has refined these techniques into a fully revised version of SING! She is author of The ABCs of Vocal Harmony book and CDs and co-author of the Born To Sing DVD. Ms. Howard has dramatically expanded the usefulness and scope of the Vocal Power Method of Singing, including new explanations and exercises for the belt voice, vibrato, breathing, singing "licks," improvisation, singing in any style and finding your own voice and identity as a singer.

Ms. Howard has trained thousands of TV, film, Broadway and recording personalities. Among the Vocal Power clients are Paige O'Hara, voice of "Belle" in the film **Beauty and the Beast**, Priscilla Presley, Demi Moore, Tony Danza, Deborah Shelton, Tanya Roberts, Lalaine, Maxine Nightingale, Stephen Dorff, Heather Tom, Kelly Packard, Christy Swanson and Drew Bell. She had ten winners on **Ed McMahon's Star Search** and contestants on **American Idol.**

Her students have appeared in musicals on Broadway and on National Tours such as **A Chorus Line, Hello Dolly**, **Follies, Good News, Peter Pan, Pippin, Jesus Christ Superstar, The Producers, Miss Saigon,** and **Phantom of the Opera,** among others. Students have also performed at **Disneyland** and **Disneyworld** as well.

Elisabeth has presented workshops world wide on the Elisabeth Howard Vocal Power Method on vocal technique and crossover styles from blues to opera in twenty cities including, Rome, Paris, Lyon, Milan, Adelaide, Oslo, Helsinki, Victoria, Rio de Janeiro, Salzburg, Innsbruck, Padua, Brescia, Firenze, Bolzano, Sassari, San Francisco, San Diego, San Jose, Los Angeles, Philadelphia, Houston and Seattle.

Elisabeth has been called a "vocal chameleon" because of her expertise in all styles of popular music and musical theater. As a singer-song writer, she had a recording contract with **MCA Music**, touring with her band. She has performed leads in numerous musicals, including **Man of La Mancha, Company, Cabaret, The Most Happy Fella, Finian's Rainbow, Jacques Brel** and others. In the classical genre, as a lyric coloratura soprano she has performed the roles of *Lucia,* in **Lucia Di Lamermoor**; the *Queen of the Night,* in the **Magic Flute**; *Sonia* in the **Merry Widow**; and *Violetta,* in **La Traviata**. In a review of her one-woman show, **Op'ra to Pop'ra** in Music Connection Magazine, she was proclaimed "*a talent to be reckoned with*."